Knit Your Own

BRITAIN

JACKIE HOLT & RUTH BAILEY

BLACK & WHITE PUBLISHING

First published 2013
by Black & White Publishing Ltd
29 Ocean Drive, Edinburgh EH6 6JL

1 3 5 7 9 10 8 6 4 2   13 14 15 16

ISBN: 978 1 84502 609 7

Design by Stuart Polson Design
Printed and bound in Poland
www.hussarbooks.pl

Contents

Introduction   1

1   William Shakespeare   3

2   Robin Hood   13

3   Henry VIII   21

4   The Beatles   31

5   James Bond   57

6   Margaret Thatcher   63

7   David and Victoria Beckham   71

8   Ant and Dec   85

9   Boris Johnson   99

10   Mini   107

11   Marmite   113

12   Cornish Pasty   117

13   Bulldog Pup   121

Glossary   126

Hints & Tips   127

Introduction

We like to think of the United Kingdom of Great Britain and Northern Ireland as a small country which has had a very big impact on the world. And our history goes back a long, long way. After the land was settled around 30,000 years ago, things were pretty quiet for a long time, although we did manage to build Stonehenge about 4,500 years back, which was a major achievement when you consider that there were no decent cranes. But things began to really hot up on our little island after the Romans arrived and brought their fancy ideas, straight roads and revolutionary plumbing. It's fair to say that they shook things up a lot in our sleepy little northern backwater, so much so that it has rarely been quiet since. The Romans didn't much like it here, not helped by dreadful weather, poor food and a large number of locals who wanted to kill them. But, typical of the Romans, they dug in and stuck at it for four centuries, albeit without ever managing to conquer anything much north of the Scottish-English border. They did get a chance to practise their wall-building skills though, resulting in Hadrian's Wall in the north of England and the Antonine Wall a little further north in central Scotland, both designed to keep the most unhappy locals at bay.

Angles, Saxons and Jutes followed later, and combined with the Picts, Britons, Scots, Celts, Norse people and others, our little island was already pretty busy and well on the way to creating a vibrant and diverse modern Britain. There was more trouble when the Normans arrived and did unspeakable things in our general direction. These French interlopers were a little haughty at first but they too ended up assimilating with the locals and bringing their own particular flavour to the party. A good deal of religious fervour followed in the Middle Ages and beyond before the political landscape we know today began to gradually emerge with the Acts of Union in 1707.

Through the centuries we've had invaders from all sort of places but it has made us who we are today and created a modern Britain which is by no means perfect but still has a lot going for it. Despite the miserable credit crunch and the last few years of relative austerity, we're still a world force economically and we have an awful lot of heritage to be proud of and to celebrate.

So why *Knit Your Own Britain*? For us, it's a celebration of the nation and a great way to reflect on the past, the present and the future of this great country. And it's also a lot of fun with, we hope, something for everyone – and they make great presents! We really hope you enjoy it as much as we have.

Jackie & Ruth

PS: We've done our very best to make sure the patterns work perfectly but please do check the website www.knityourownbritain.co.uk for updates and minor amends or additional explanations. Enjoy!

You will need

MATERIALS:
Colour Codes:
1 Rowan Baby Merino Silk DK (Shade 00674 – Shell Pink) – For Body
2 Debbie Bliss Rialto 4-Ply (Shade 22018 – Teal Blue) – For Coat
3 Debbie Bliss Rialto Lace (Shade 44012 – Oatmeal) – For Shirt & Legs
4 Rowan Fine Tweed (Shade 373 – Brown) – For Boots
5 Rowan Pure Life British Sheep Breeds Fine Boucle (Shade 00318 – Dark Masham) – For Hair, Beard & Moustache

Embroidery thread – 2 hanks in different tones of Brown for Hair
7 beads as buttons
Beads for eyes
Stuffing

NEEDLES:
Size 10/3.25mm
Size 11/3.00mm
Size 12/2.75mm
Size 12/2.75mm double-ended
Size 13/2.25mm
Crochet hook 1.75mm
Darning needle

William Shakespeare

Who better to start off our mini British journey with than the bard himself, William Shakespeare, who has given the world such a rich legacy? When we consider how much he wrote and the quality of his work, it is amazing that so little is known about his own life. Born in the 1560s in Stratford-upon-Avon, young Will must have been a precocious child as his genius developed. He married Anne Hathaway when he was just eighteen years old and they had three children. Then, in his twenties, he discovered that all the world was a stage, and all the men and women merely players who had their exits and their entrances. With that, he exited Stratford and headed to the bright candles of London to begin his career as an actor and writer.

Companies of players in London were nothing unusual, and William was soon involved in his own venture, no doubt writing furiously to attract an audience in a very competitive industry. He soon found he had a talent for comedies and histories which brought him an audience and fame, and he later moved on to tragedies like *Macbeth* and *Hamlet*. But he was not without enemies, who saw him as an upstart who had no business being more successful than his upper class, university-educated rivals. His career and talents brought him a comfortable fortune, particularly after his involvement with the Globe theatre, and his work later afforded him a very good life before his death in 1616 at the age of fifty-two.

Although Shakespeare's work was published during his lifetime, it was much later before it was fully appreciated for its true genius, and the Victorians did much to help his reputation. His best work will be a part of the fabric of our lives forever, with so many phrases in daily use. We beware the Ides of March; we fight fire with fire; we know the green-eyed monster; we give the Devil his due; stiffen the sinews; we sleep, perchance to dream; and we wear our hearts on our sleeves until, when we have seen better days, we shuffle off this mortal coil. Forsooth, there was method in his madness!

BODY

COLOUR I
- Size 10/3.25mm needles

BODY –FRONT
- Cast on 16
- 1st row: K
- 2nd row: P
- 3rd row: K1, inc in next, K12, inc in next, K1 (18sts)
- Work 3 rows SS starting with P
- 7th row: K1, K2tog, K2, K2tog, K4, K2tog, K2, K2tog, K1 (14sts)
- Work 3 rows SS starting with P
- 11th row: K2, inc in next, K8, inc in next, K2 (16sts)
- 12th row: P
- 13th row: Inc in 1st, K3, inc in next, K6, inc in next, K3, inc in last (20sts)
- Work 7 rows SS starting with P
- 21st row: K1, sl1, K1, psso, K14, K2tog, K (18sts)
- Work 5 rows SS starting with P
- 27th row: K1, sl1, K1, psso, K12, K2tog, K1 (16sts)
- 28th row: P1, P2tog, P10, P2tog, P1 (14sts)
- 29th row: K1, sl1, K1, psso, K8, K2tog, K1 (12sts)
- 30th row: P
- Cast off

BODY – BACK
- Cast on 16
- 1st row: K
- 2nd row: P
- 3rd row: K2, inc in next, K1, inc in next, K6, inc in next, K1, inc in next, K2 (20sts)
- 4th row: P
- 5th row: K3, inc in next, K1, inc in next, K8, inc in next, K1, inc in next, K3 (24sts)
- 6th row: P16, turn –

- 7th row: K8, turn –
- 8th row: P10, turn –
- 9th row: K12, turn –
- 10th row: P18
- 11th row: K24
- 12th row: P24
- 13th row: K1, K2tog, K18, K2tog, K1 (22sts)
- 14th row: P
- 15th row: K2, K2tog, K1, K2tog, K8, K2tog, K1, K2tog, K2 (18sts)
- 16th row: P
- 17th row: K2, K2tog, K2, K2tog, K2, K2tog, K2, K2tog, K2 (14sts)
- Work 5 rows SS starting with P
- 23rd row: K1, inc in next, K4, inc in next, inc in next, K4, inc in next, K1 (18sts)
- Work 11 rows SS starting with P
- 35th row: K1, sl1, K1, psso, K12, K2tog, K1 (16sts)
- 36th row: P1, P2tog, P10, P2tog, P1 (14sts)
- 37th row: K1, sl1, K1, psso, K8, K2tog, K1 (12sts)
- 38th row: P
- Cast off

To make up: Join front to back. Stuff.

ARMS – MAKE TWO

COLOUR I
- Size 10/3.25mm needles

WORKING FROM SHOULDER TO WRIST
- Cast on 5
- 1st row: K
- 2nd row: P
- 3rd row K1, inc in next, K1, inc in next, K1 (7sts)
- 4th row: P
- 5th row: K1, inc in next, K3, inc in next, K1 (9sts)

- 6th row: P
- 7th row: K4, inc in next, K4 (10sts)
- Work 13 rows SS starting with P
- 21st row: K2tog, K6, K2tog (8sts)
- 22nd row: P2tog, P4, P2tog (6sts)
- 23rd row: K1, inc in next, K2, inc in next, K1 (8sts)
- Work 7 rows SS starting with P
- 31st row: K3, K2tog, K3 (7sts)
- Work 3 rows SS starting with P
- 35th row: K1, sl1, K1, psso, K1, K2tog, K1 (5sts)
- 36th row: P
- 37th row: K1, inc in next, K1, inc in next, K1 (7sts)
- 38th row: P
- 39th row: K1, inc in next, K3, inc in next, K1 (9sts)
- 40th row: P

FOR LEFT HAND
- 41st row: K2, put 2sts on pin, K5 (7sts)
- Work 3 rows SS starting with P
- 45th row: K2tog, K2tog, K2tog, K1 (4sts)
- 46th row: P2tog, P2tog (2sts)
- Pull wool through

FOR RIGHT HAND
- 41st row: K5, put 2sts on pin, K2 (7sts)
- Work 3 rows SS starting with P
- 45th row: K1, K2tog, K2tog, K2tog (4sts)
- 46th row: P2tog, P2tog (2sts)
- Pull wool through

THUMBS – SAME FOR BOTH HANDS
- Join wool to 2sts on pin
- Use 12/2.75mm double-ended to work i-cord for 3 rows.
- Pull wool through and darn end

To make up: Join seams. Stuff. Attach to body.

LEGS

COLOUR 3 – USE AS DOUBLE THREAD

- Size 11/3.00mm needles

- Cast on 24
- 1st row: K
- 2nd row: P
- 3rd row: K10, K2tog, K2tog, K10 (22sts)
- 4th row: P10, P2tog, P10 (21sts)
- 5th row: K5, (K2tog, K1)x3, K2tog, K5 (17sts)
- 6th row: P
- 7th row: K4, cast off 8, K4 (9sts)
- 8th row: P, pulling 2 sections together
- Work 6 rows SS starting with K
- 15th row: K1, inc in next, K5, inc in next, K1 (11sts)
- Work 3 rows SS starting with P
- 19th row: K1, inc in next, K7, inc in next, K1 (13sts)
- Work 3 rows SS starting with P
- 23rd row: K1, inc in next, K9, inc in next, K1 (15sts)
- 24th row: P
- 25th row: K1, inc in next, K11, inc in next, K1 (17sts)
- Work 3 rows SS starting with P
- 29th row: K1, sl1, K1, psso, K11, K2tog, K1 (15sts)
- 30th row: P1, P2tog, P9, P2tog, P1 (13sts)
- 31st row: K1, sl1, K1, psso, K7, K2tog, K1 (11sts)
- Work 3 rows SS starting with P
- 35th row: K1, inc in next, K7, inc in next, K1 (13sts)
- Work 3 rows SS starting with P
- 39th row: K1, inc in next, K9, inc in next, K1 (15sts)

- Work 3 rows SS starting with P
- 43rd row: K1, inc in next, K11, inc in next, K1 (17sts)
- Work 3 rows SS starting with P
- 47h row: K1, inc in next, K13, inc in next, K1 (19sts)
- Work 3 rows SS starting with P
- 51st row: K1, inc in next, K15, inc in next, K1 (21sts)
- Work 11 rows SS starting with P
- Cast off

To make up: Join seams. Stuff. Attach to body.

HEAD

COLOUR 1

- Size 10/3.25mm needles

HEAD – BACK

- Cast on 6
- 1st row: K
- 2nd row: P
- 3rd row: K1, inc in next, K2, inc in next, K1 (8sts)
- Work 3 rows SS starting with P
- 7th row: K1, inc in next, K4, inc in next, K1 (10sts)
- 8th row: P
- 9th row: K3, inc in next, K2, inc in next, K3 (12sts)
- 10th row: P
- 11th row: K2, (inc in next)x3, K2, (inc in next)x3, K2 (18sts)
- Work 3 rows SS starting with P
- 15th row: K4, (inc in next, K2)x3, inc in next, K4 (22sts)
- Work 3 rows SS starting with P
- 19th row: K1, sl1, K1, psso, K2, (sl1, K1, psso)x2, K4, (K2tog)x2, K2, K2tog, K1 (16sts)
- 20th row: P
- 21st row: K1, (sl1, K1, psso)x3, (K2tog)x4, K1 (8sts)

- 2nd row: P
- Cast off

HEAD – FRONT (RIGHT SIDE)

- Cast on 5
- 1st row: K
- 2nd row: P
- 3rd row: Cast on 2, K to end (7sts)
- 4th row: P5, inc in next, inc in next (9sts)
- 5th row: K1, inc in next, inc in next, K6 (11sts)
- 6th row: P11 – break wool, leave sts on needle

HEAD – FRONT (LEFT SIDE)

- With WS facing cast on 5, turn –
- Now working on these 5sts only:
- 1st row: K
- 2nd row: P
- 3rd row: K, cast on 2 (7sts)
- 4th row: P1, inc in next, inc in next, P4 (9sts)
- 5th row: K6, inc in next, inc in next, K1 (11sts)
- 6th row: P11
- 7th row: K across 2 pieces to join, K10, K2tog, K10 (21sts)
- 8th row: P1, P2tog, P15, P2tog, P1 (19sts)
- Work 6 rows SS starting with K
- 15th row: K1, sl1, K1, psso, K13, K2tog, K1 (17sts)
- 16th row: P
- 17th row: K1, sl1, K1, psso, K11, K2tog, K1 (15sts)
- 18th row: P
- 19th row: K1, sl1, K1, psso, K9, K2tog, K1 (13sts)
- 20th row: P1, P2tog, P7, P2tog, P1 (11sts)
- 21st row: K1, sl1, K1, psso, K5, K2tog, K1 (9sts)
- 22nd row: P
- Cast off

To make up: Join seam under chin. Join front and back together. Stuff. Attach to body.

BREECHES

COLOUR 2

- Size 12/2.75mm needles

LEFT LEG

- Cast on 18
- Work 3 rows SS starting with K
- 4th row: P1, P2tog, P12, P2tog, P1 (16sts)
- 5th row: K1, sl1, K1, psso, K10, K2tog, K1 (14sts)
- Work 3 rows SS starting with P
- 9th row: K1, inc in next, K10, inc in next, K1 (16sts)
- Work 3 rows SS starting with P
- 13th row: K1, inc in next, K12, inc in next, K1 (18sts)
- 14th row: P
- 15th row: K6, inc in next, K4, inc in next, K6 (20sts)
- 16th row: P
- 17th row: K1, inc in next, K16, inc in next, K1 (22sts)
- 18th row: P
- 19th row: K7, inc in next, K6, inc in next, K7 (24sts)
- 20th row: P
- 21st row: K1, inc in next, K7, inc in next, K4, inc in next, K7, inc in next, K1 (28sts)
- 22nd row: P
- 23rd row: K9, inc in next, K8, inc in next, K9 (30sts)
- 24th row: P
- 25th row: K1, inc in next, K9, inc in next, K6, inc in next, K9, inc in next, K1 (34sts)
- 26th row: P
- 27th row: K1, inc in next, K9, inc in next, K10, inc in next, K9, inc in next, K1 (38sts)
- 28th row: P
- 29th row: K1, inc in next, K9, inc in next, K6, inc in next, K7, inc in next, K9, inc in next, K1 (43sts)
- 30th row: P
- 31st row: K14, inc in next, K13, inc in next, K14 (45sts)
- Work 6 rows SS starting with P
- 38th row: Cast off 3, P to end (42sts)
- 39th row: Cast off 3, K to end (39sts)
- Put sts on pin

RIGHT LEG

- Cast on 18
- Repeat rows 1 to 39 (above)

TO JOIN LEGS TOGETHER

- 40th row: P38 from right leg, P2tog (last st of right with 1st of left), P38 from left (77sts)
- 41st row: K2tog, K3, inc in next, K7, inc in next, K6, inc in next, K6, inc in next, K7, inc in next, K5, inc in next, K7, inc in next, K6, inc in next, K6, inc in next, K7, inc in next, K3, K2tog (85sts)
- Work 3 rows SS starting with P
- 45th row: K5, inc in next, K8, inc in next, K7, inc in next, K7, inc in next, K8, inc in next, K5, inc in next, K8, inc in next, K7, inc in next, K7, inc in next, K8, inc in next, K5 (95sts)
- Work 2 rows SS starting with P
- 48th row: P25, turn –
- 49th row: K25
- 50th row: P15, turn –
- 51st row: K15
- 52nd row: P
- 53rd row: K25, turn –
- 54th row: P25
- 55th row: K15, turn –
- 56th row: P15
- 57th row: (K1, K2tog)x14, K11, (K2tog, K1)x14 (67sts)
- 58th row: P
- 59th row: (K1, K2tog)x4, (K2tog) x2, (K1, K2tog)x4, K11, (K2tog, K1)x4, (K2tog)x2, (K2tog, K1)x4 (47sts)
- Work 4 rows SS starting with P
- Cast off

To make up: Sew inside leg seams and through crotch. Dress doll.

SHIRT

Note: This is a U-shaped piece which fits around the back of the neck, over the shoulders and down the front of the doll.

COLOUR 3

- Size 12/2.75mm needles

- Cast on 35
- Work 12 rows GS
- 13th row: Cast off 27, K7 (8sts)
- Work 13 rows GS – leave on needle
- On second needle cast on 27sts
- K8 from first needle to join pieces together (35sts)
- Work 12 rows GS
- Cast off

SHIRT COLLAR

- Pick-up 6sts from left side, 6sts from back, 6sts from right side (18sts)
- Work 3 rows GS
- 4th row: K2, inc in next, K2, inc in next, K6, inc in next, K2, inc in next, K2 (22sts)
- 5th row: K2, inc in next, K2, inc in next, K10, inc in next, K2, inc in next, K2 (26sts)
- 6th row: K
- 7th row: K9, turn –
- 8th row: K9
- 9th row: K

- 10th row: K9, turn –
- 11th row: K9
- Cast off loosely
- With 1.75mm crochet hook work chain loops around outside edge of collar.

To make up: Place around neck of doll. Catch in place at centre-front.

SHIRT SLEEVE CUFF DETAIL – MAKE TWO

COLOUR 3
- Size 12/2.75mm needles

- Cast on 24 loosely
- Work 11 rows GS
- Cast off

To make up: Join short edges. Sew on inside of sleeves so that this shows just below the cuff.

BOOTS

COLOUR 4
- Size 12/2.75mm needles

LEFT BOOT
- Cast on 6
- Work 3 rows SS starting with P
- 4th row: K1, inc in next, K2, inc in next, K1   (8sts)
- 5th row: P
- 6th row: K1, inc in next, K4, inc in next, K1   (10sts)
- 7th row: P
- 8th row: K1, inc in next, K6, inc in next, K1   (12sts)
- 9th row: P
- 10th row: K1, inc in next, K8, inc in next, K1   (14sts)
- 11th row: P
- 12th row: K

- 13th row: P1, P2tog, P8, P2tog, P1 (12sts)
- 14th row: K1, K2tog, K6, K2tog, K1 (10sts)
- 15th row: P
- 16th row: K1, inc in next, K6, inc in next, K1   (12sts)
- 17th row: P5, turn –
- 18th row: K2tog, K3   (4sts)
- Work 4 rows SS starting with P
- 23rd row: P2tog, P2   (3sts)
- Cast off 3
- Put next 2sts onto pin
- Work on remaining 5sts
- 17th row continued: P5
- 18th row: K3, K2tog   (4sts)
- Work 3 rows SS starting with P
- 22nd row: K2tog, K2   (3sts)
- Cast off 3
- Pull wool through
- With RS facing pick-up 5sts from outside ankle, K2 from pin, pick-up 6sts from inside ankle   (13sts)
- 1st row: P
- 2nd row: K
- 3rd row: P2, P2tog, P5, P2tog, P2 (11sts)
- 4th row: K
- 5th row: K1, P to last, K1
- Repeat rows 4 and 5 (x2)
- 10th row: K1, inc in next, K2, K2tog, K3, inc in next, K1   (12sts)
- 11th row: K1, P to last, K1
- 12th row: K
- 13th row: K1, P to last, K1
- 14th row: K2, inc in next, K6, inc in next, K2   (14sts)
- 15th row: K1, P to last, K1
- 16th row: K3, inc in next, K2, K2tog, K2, inc in next, K3   (15sts)
- 17th row: K1, P to last, K1
- 18th row: K4, inc in next, K5, inc in next, K4   (17sts)
- 19th row: K1, P to last, K1

- 20th row: K4, inc in next, K2, K2tog, K3, inc in next, K4   (18sts)
- 21st row: K1, P to last, K1
- 22nd row: K4, inc in next, K8, inc in next, K4   (20sts)
- 23rd row: K1, P to last, K1
- 24th row: K
- 25th row: K1, P to last, K1
- 26th row: K4, K2tog, K8, K2tog, K4 (18sts)
- 27th row: K1, P2, P2tog, P8, P2tog, P2, K1   (16sts)
- 28th row: K3, K2tog, K6, K2tog, K3 (14sts) – Mark with tag
- 29th row: K2, P to last 2sts, K2
- 30th row: K1, (K1, inc in next)x3, (inc in next, K1)x3, K1   (20sts)
- 31st row: K2, P to last 2sts, K2
- 32nd row: K3, inc in next, K5, inc in next, K6, inc in next, K3   (23sts)
- 33rd row: K2, P to last 2sts, K2
- 34th row: K2tog, cast off to last 2sts, K2tog
- Pull wool through

RIGHT BOOT
- Cast on 6
- Work 3 rows SS starting with P
- 4th row: K1, inc in next, K2, inc in next, K1   (8sts)
- 5th row: P
- 6th row: K1, inc in next, K4, inc in next, K1   (10sts)
- 7th row: P
- 8th row: K1, inc in next, K6, inc in next, K1   (12sts)
- 9th row: P
- 10th row: K1, inc in next, K8, inc in next, K1   (14sts)
- 11th row: P
- 12th row: K
- 13th row: P1, P2tog, P8, P2tog, P1 (12sts)
- 14th row: K1, K2tog, K6, K2tog, K1 (10sts)

- 15th row: P
- 16th row: K1, inc in next, K6, inc in next, K1   (12sts)
- 17th row: P5, turn –
- 18th row: K2tog, K3   (4sts)
- Work 3 rows SS starting with P
- 22nd row: K2, K2tog   (3sts)
- Cast off 3
- Pull wool through
- Put next 2sts on pin
- Work on remaining 5sts
- 17th row continued: P5
- 18th row: K3, K2tog   (4sts)
- Work 4 rows SS starting with P
- 23rd row: P2, P2tog   (3sts)
- Cast off 3 – use last sts as 1st of next row
- With RS facing pick-up 5sts from inside ankle, K2 from pin, pick-up 5sts from outside ankle   (13sts)
- 1st row: P
- 2nd row: K
- 3rd row: P2, P2tog, P5, P2tog, P2   (11sts)
- 4th row: K
- 5th row: K1, P to last, K1
- Repeat rows 4 and 5 (x2)
- 10th row: K1, inc in next, K2, sl1, K1, psso, K3, inc in next, K1   (12sts)
- 11th row: K1, P to last, K1
- 12th row: K
- 13th row: K1, P to last, K1
- 14th row: K2, inc in next, K6, inc in next, K2   (14sts)
- 15th row: K1, P to last, K1
- 16th row: K3, inc in next, K2, sl1, K1, psso, K2, inc in next, K3   (15sts)
- 17th row: K1, P to last, K1
- 18th row: K4, inc in next, K5, inc in next, K4   (17sts)
- 19th row: K1, P to last, K1
- 20th row: K4, inc in next, K3, sl1, K1, psso, K2, inc in next, K4   (18sts)
- 21st row: K1, P to last, K1

- 22nd row: K4, inc in next, K8, inc in next, K4   (20sts)
- 23rd row: K1, P to last, K1
- 24th row: K
- 25th row: K1, P to last, K1
- 26th row: K4, sl1, K1, psso, K8, sl1, K1, psso, K4   (18sts)
- 27th row: K1, P2, P2tog, P8, P2tog, P2, K1   (16sts)
- 28th row: K3, sl1, K1, psso, K6, sl1, K1, psso, K3   (14sts) – Mark with tag
- 29th row: K2, P to last 2sts, K2
- 30th row: K1, (K1, inc in next)x3, (inc in next, K1)x3, K1   (20sts)
- 31st row: K2, P to last 2sts, K2
- 32nd row: K3, inc in next, K6, inc in next, K5, inc in next, K3   (23sts)
- 33rd row: K2, P to last 2sts, K2
- 34th row: K2tog, cast off to last 2sts, K2tog
- Pull wool through

To make up: Sew-up from toe, under foot, around heel to just above the ankle. Put on doll. Lace up centre-back to just below tag and tie off. The cuff of the boot stands up over the knee.

DOUBLET

COLOUR 2
- Size 12/2.75mm needles

DOUBLET – BACK
- Cast on 24
- Work 3 rows SS starting with P
- Work 2 rows K
- 6th row: K1, inc in next, K19, inc in next, K1   (26sts)
- Work 3 rows P
- 10th row: K1, inc in next, K21, inc in next, K1   (28sts)
- 11th row: P
- Work 3 rows K
- Work 3 rows P

- 18th row: K
- 19th row: P
- Work 2 rows K
- 22nd row: Cast off 2, K to end   (26sts)
- 23rd row: Cast off 2, P3, K1, P2, K1, P8, K1, P2, K1, P3, K1   (24sts)
- 24th row: K1, P1, K3, P1, K2, P1, K6, P1, K2, P1, K3, P1, K1
- 25th row: P2, K1, P3, K1, P2, K1, P4, K1, P2, K1, P3, K1, P2
- 26th row: K3, P1, K3, P1, K2, P1, K2, P1, K2, P1, K3, P1, K3
- 27th row: P4, K1, P3, K1, P2, K2, P2, K1, P3, K1, P4
- 28th row: K5, P1, K3, P1, K4, P1, K3, P1, K5
- 29th row: P6, K1, P3, K1, P2, K1, P3, K1, P6
- 30th row: P8, K3, P2, K3, P8
- 31st row: P1, P2tog, P2, P2tog, P1, K1, P6, K1, P1, P2tog, P2, P2tog, P1   (20sts)
- 32nd row: K7, P1, K4, P1, K7
- 33rd row: P8, K1, P2, K1, P8
- 34th row: K9, P2, K9
- 35th row: P6, P2tog, P4, P2tog, P6   (18sts)
- 36th row: Cast off 3, P14   (15sts)
- 37th row: Cast off 3, P11   (12sts)
- 38th row: Cast off 3, K8   (9sts)
- 39th row: Cast off 3, P5   (6st)
- Put on pin

DOUBLET – LEFT FRONT
- Cast on 14
- 1st row: K
- 2nd row: K1, P9, turn –
- 3rd row: K10
- 4th row: K1, P13
- 5th row: K
- 6th row: K1, P8, turn –
- 7th row: K9
- 8th row: K1, P to end

- 9th row: P13, K1
- 10th row: K1, P11, inc in next, P1 (15sts)
- Work 3 rows K
- 14th row: K1, P12, inc in next, P1 (16sts)
- 15th row: K
- 16th row: K1, P to end
- 17th row: P15, K1
- 18th row: K1, P to end
- Work 3 rows K
- 22nd row: K1, P to end
- Work 2 rows K
- 25th row: Cast off 3, K to end (13sts)
- 26th row: K1, P4, K1, P2, K1, P3, K1
- 27th row: K1, P1, K3, P1, K2, P1, K4
- 28th row: K1, P2, K1, P2, K1, P3, K1, P2
- 29th row: P1, K2, P1, K3, P1, K2, P1, K2
- 30th row: K2, P2, K1, P3, K1, P2, K1, P1
- 31st row: K2, P1, K2, P1, K3, P1, K3
- 32nd row: K1, P1, K1, P3, K1, P2, K1, P3
- 33rd row: K4, P1, K2, P1, K3, P1, K1
- 34th row: K1, P3, K1, P2, K1, P5
- 35th row: K6, P1, K2, P1, K3
- 36th row: K1, P1, K1, P2, K1, P7
- 37th row: Cast off 3, K4, P1, K2, P1, K1 (10sts)
- 38th row: K1, P2, K1, P6
- 39th row: Cast off 3, K3, P1, K2 (7sts)
- Put on pin

DOUBLET – RIGHT FRONT
- Cast on 14
- 1st row: P to last, K1
- 2nd row: K10, turn –
- 3rd row: P9, K1
- 4th row: K14
- 5th row: P13, K1
- 6th row: K9, turn –
- 7th row: P8, K1
- Work 2 rows K
- 10th row: K12, inc in next, K1 (15sts)
- 11th row: P to last, K1

- 12th row: K1, P to end
- 13th row: P to last, K1
- 14th row: K13, inc in next, K1 (16sts)
- 15th row: P to last, K1
- Work 3 rows K
- 19th row: P to last, K1
- 20th row: K1, P to end
- 21st row: P to last, K1
- 22nd row: K
- 23rd row: P to last, K1
- 24th row: K1, P to end
- 25th row: Cast off 3, P11, K1 (13sts)
- 26th row: K5, P1, K2, P1, K3, P1
- 27th row: P1, K1, P3, K1, P2, K1, P3, K1
- 28th row: K3, P1, K2, P1, K3, P1, K2
- 29th row: K1, P2, K1, P3, K1, P2, K1, P1, K1
- 30th row: K1, P1, K2, P1, K3, P1, K2, P1, K1
- 31st row: P2, K1, P2, K1, P3, K1, P2, K1
- 32nd row: K2, P1, K3, P1, K2, P1, K3
- 33rd row: P4, K1, P2, K1, P3, K2
- 34th row: K4, P1, K2, P1, K5
- 35th row: P6, K1, P2, K1, P2, K1
- 36th row: K2, P1, K2, P1, K7
- 37th row: Cast off 3, P4, K1, P2, K2 (10sts)
- 38th row: K3, P1, K6
- 39th row: Cast off 3, P3, K1, P1, K1 (7sts)
- Join shoulder seams

TO CREATE COLLAR
- With RS facing starting at right centre front
- Working on 20st (7st right front neck, 6st back neck, 7st left front neck):
- 1st row: K1, inc in next, K1, inc in next, K2, inc in next 2, K1, inc in next 2, K1, inc in next 2, K2, inc in next, K1, inc in next, K1 (30sts)
- 2nd row: K1, P to last, K1
- 3rd row: K24, turn –
- 4th row: P18, turn –

- 5th row: K24
- 6th row: K1, P21, turn –
- 7th row: Inc in 1st, K4, inc in next, K2, inc in next, K4, inc in next, turn –
- 8th row: P18, turn –
- 9th row: K26
- 10th row: K1, P to last, K1 (34sts)
- 11th row: K
- Cast off

TABS AT WAIST OF DOUBLET – MAKE TEN
WORKING FROM HEM TO WAIST
- Cast on 9
- Work 3 rows K
- 4th row: K2, P5, K2
- 5th row: K
- 6th row: K1, K2tog, P3, K2tog, K1 (7sts)
- 7th row: K
- 8th row: K2, P3, K2
- 9th row: K2, K2tog, K3 (6sts)
- 10th row: K2, P2, K2
- 11th row: K2, K2tog, K2 (5sts)
- Cast off

DOUBLET SLEEVES – MAKE TWO
- Cast on 20
- Work 3 rows K
- 4th row: K1, K2tog, P4, P2tog, P2, P2tog, P4, K2tog, K1 (16sts)
- 5th row: K
- 6th row: K2, P12, K2
- 7th row: K1, inc in next, K12, inc in next, K1 (18sts)
- To close the vent and create the underarm seam, put stitches onto 3 needles. Join into circle.
- 8th row: K9, turn –
- 9th row: P18, turn –
- 10th row: K18, turn
- 11th row: P18, turn –

- 12th row: K18, turn –
- 13th row: K18 – The work should now be flat enough to work on two needles
- 14th row: K1, inc in next, K14, inc in next, K1 (20sts)
- Work 3 rows P
- 18th row: K1, P1, K3, P1, K8, P1, K3, P1, K1
- 19th row: P2, K1, P3, K1, P6, K1, P3, K1, P2
- 20th row: P1, K2, P1, K3, P1, K4, P1, K3, P1, K2, P1
- 21st row: P1, K1, P2, K1, P3, K1, P2, K1, P3, K1, P2, K1, P1
- 22nd row: K1, inc in next, P1, K2, P1, K3, P2, K3, P1, K2, P1, inc in next, K1
- 23rd row: P4, K1, P2, K1, P6, K1, P2, K1, P4
- 24th row: P1, K4, P1, K2, P1, K4, P1, K2, P1, K4, P1
- 25th row: P1, K1, P4, K1, P2, K1, P2, K1, P2, K1, P4, K1, P1
- 26th row: K2, P1, K4, P1, K2, P2, K2, P1, K4, P1, K2
- 27th row: K1, P2, K1, P4, K1, P4, K1, P4, K1, P2, K1
- 28th row: K1, inc in next, K2, P1, K4, P1, K2, P1, K4, P1, K2, inc in next, K1 (24sts)
- 29th row: P3, K1, P2, K1, P4, K2, P4, K1, P2, K1, P3
- 30th row: K4, P1, K2, P1, K8, P1, K2, P1, K4
- 31st row: P5, K1, P2, K1, P6, K1, P2, K1, P5
- 32nd row: K1, inc in next, K4, P1, K2, P1, K4, P1, K2, P1, K4, inc in next, K1 (26sts)
- 33rd row: P8, K1, P2, K1, P2, K1, P2, K1, P8
- 34th row: P10, K2, P2, K2, P10
- 35th row: P10, K1, P4, K1, P10
- 36th row: K11, P1, K2, P1, K11

- 37th row: P12, K2, P12
- Work 2 rows P
- Work 2 rows K
- 42nd row: Cast off 3, K to end (23sts)
- 43rd row: Cast off 3, P to end (20sts)
- 44th row: K
- 45th row: P
- 46th row: K1, sl1, K1, psso, K4, sl1, K1, psso, K2, K2tog, K4, K2tog, K1 (16sts)
- 47th row: P1, P2tog, P10, P2tog, P1 (14sts)
- 48th row: K1, sl1, K1, psso, K8, K2tog, K1 (12sts)
- Cast off

EPAULETTES – MAKE TWO

- Cast on 3
- WORKING IN GS:
- Work 3 rows
- 4th row: K1, inc in next, K1 (4sts)
- 5th row: K
- 6th row: K1, inc in next, K2 (5sts)
- 7th row: K
- 8th row: K1, inc in next, K3 (6sts)
- 9th row: K
- 10th row: K1, inc in next, K4 (7sts)
- 11th row: K
- 12th row: K1, inc in next, K5 (8sts)
- 13th row: K
- 14th row: K1, inc in next, K6 (9sts)
- 15th row: K
- 16th row: K6, turn –
- 17th row: K6
- 18th row: K7, turn –
- 19th row: K7
- 20th row: K6, turn –
- 21st row: K6
- Work 2 rows K
- 24th row: K1, sl1, K1, psso, K6 (8sts)
- 25th row: K
- 26th row; K1, sl1, K1, psso, K5 (7sts)

- 27th row: K
- 28th row: K1, sl1, K1, psso, K4 (6sts)
- 29th row: K
- 30th row: K1, sl1, K1, psso, K3 (5sts)
- 31st row: K
- 32nd row: K1, sl1, K1, psso, K2 (4sts)
- 33rd row: K
- 34th row: K1, sl1, K1, psso, K1 (3sts)
- Work 3 rows K
- Cast off

To make up Doublet: Join side seams. Join sleeve seams and inset. Sew tabs evenly around bottom of Doublet. Sew epaulettes to armhole seam using the longer, narrower end at front, lining up to the top rib of Doublet back and front. Catch centre-back of collar to nape of Doublet to allow the back section of the collar to roll. Dress doll. Pull lace collar of shirt over the Doublet collar. If necessary, catch front points of collar to Doublet to lie flat. Sew-up Doublet to chest. Add 7 beads as buttons.

HAIR

To make the embroidery thread crinkly, knit approx. $2/3$ of each hank on 2.25mm needles and steam press. Unravel and set aside. Using COLOUR 5 work in close zigzag lines from nape to crown, to cover head completely. Stitch lengths of the curly embroidery thread in random loose scribbles over the top of the brown yarn. This is applied where the hair would be worn longest. Finish by knotting in some short lengths of the two embroidery threads to the front hairline and cut short to create a standing fringe.

NOSE

COLOUR 1
- Size 13/2.25mm needles
- Cast on 6
- 1st row: K
- 2nd row: P1, P2tog, P1   (4sts)
- 3rd row: K
- 4th row: P1, P2tog, P1   (3sts)
- 5th row: K3
- Pull thread through 3sts

To make up: Attach to face.

TO CREATE FACE

The beard, moustache and eyebrows are stitched directly to the face in COLOUR 5. If you want to you can mix in a few strands of embroidery thread. Ears are crochet chains stitched on. Add beads for eyes. Add mouth in yarn of choice.

PEN

Goose feathers are used for quills, but we found a 9cm white swan's feather near a duck pond! Strip all of the down from lower shaft and trim the feathers to a neat shape. Cut nib at angle. Stitch into his hand.

You will need

MATERIALS:

Colour Codes:
1 Rowan Baby Merino Silk DK
(Shade 00674 – Shell Pink) – For Body
2 Debbie Bliss Rialto Lace
(Shade 44012 – Cream) – Use as
double thread – For Legs
3 Rowan Fine Tweed (Shade 360 –
Oatmeal) – For Breeches
4 Debbie Bliss Rialto Lace (Shade
44002 – Pale Grey) – For Shirt
5 Rowan Fine Tweed
(Shade 370 – Green) – For Blanket
6 Debbie Bliss Baby Cashmerino
(Shade 340011 – Brown) – For Cape
7 Patons 100% Cotton (Shade 2712 –
Black) – For Belt & Quiver

Fine wool & charcoal black embroi-
dery thread for hair
Beads for eyes
Gold wire for buckle
Kebab skewers
Thick cotton twine
Piece of twig/cane
18cm piece of plastic boning
Hot-fix studs
Fine millinery/craft wire
Fine cord
Plasti-Kote Fast-Dry Enamel
in gold leaf
Glue
Stuffing

NEEDLES:
Size 10/3.25mm
Size 10/3.25mm double-ended
Size 11/3.00mm
Size 12/2.75mm
Size 12/2.75mm double-ended
Size 13/2.25mm
Crochet hook 2.50mm
Darning needle

Robin Hood

Robin Hood and his Merry Men are part of the Lincoln green fabric of the nation. Since medieval times the legend of Robin Hood has grown and developed, to the point where it is now difficult to tell fact from fiction. A renowned archer, an outlaw, a dispossessed aristocrat fighting the oppression of the evil King John, a friend of Richard the Lionheart and a man who robbed from the rich to give to the poor, Robin was clearly very busy in his Sherwood Forest home near Nottingham. His Merry Men also have a treasured place in our hearts. Little John, Friar Tuck, Will Scarlet, Alan A'Dale and Much the Miller's Son all appear in the story of Robin Hood, along with his love interest, the enigmatic and beautiful Maid Marian.

Whatever the truth of the story, Robin Hood and his Merry Men stand for good against evil, as the Sheriff of Nottingham fills his coffers at the expense of the ordinary folk of England and does the bidding of wicked King John. Hollywood and television have long had a fascination with the legend, and from the earliest movie in 1908, actors such as Douglas Fairbanks, Errol Flynn, Sean Connery, Michael Praed, Jason Connery and Russell Crowe have taken on the role, with varying success. Just why have so many famous actors played him, you might ask? Well, it must be down to the enduring popularity of his story and the fact that in true hero fashion he fought the baddies and took from the rich to give to the poor.

BODY

COLOUR I
- Size 10/3.25mm needles

FRONT BODY
- Cast on 16
- 1st row: K
- 2nd row: P
- 3rd row: K1, inc in next, K12, inc in next, K1   (18sts)
- Work 3 rows SS starting with P
- 7th row: K1, K2tog, K2, K2tog, K4, K2tog, K2, K2tog, K1   (14sts)
- Work 3 rows SS starting with P
- 11th row: K2, inc in next, K8, inc in next, K2   (16sts)
- 12th row: P
- 13th row: Inc in 1st, K3, inc in next, K6, inc in next, K3, inc in last   (20sts)
- Work 7 rows SS starting with P
- 21st row: K1, sl1, K1, psso, K14, K2tog, K   (18sts)
- Work 5 rows SS starting with P
- 27th row: K1, sl1, K1, psso, K12, K2tog, K1   (16sts)
- 28th row: P1, P2tog, P10, P2tog, P1   (14sts)
- 29th row: K1, sl1, K1, psso, K8, K2tog, K1   (12sts)
- 30th row: P
- Cast off

BODY – BACK
- Cast on 16
- 1st row: K
- 2nd row: P
- 3rd row: K2, inc in next, K1, inc in next, K6, inc in next, K1, inc in next, K2   (20sts)
- 4th row: P
- 5th row: K3, inc in next, K1, inc in next, K8, inc in next, K1, inc in next, K3   (24sts)
- 6th row: P16, turn –

- 7th row: K8, turn –
- 8th row: P10, turn –
- 9th row: K12, turn –
- 10th row: P18
- 11th row: K24
- 12th row: P24
- 13th row: K1, K2tog, K18, K2tog, K1   (22sts)
- 14th row: P
- 15th row: K2, K2tog, K1, K2tog, K8, K2tog, K1, K2tog, K2   (18sts)
- 16th row: P
- 17th row: K2, K2tog, K2, K2tog, K2, K2tog, K2, K2tog, K2   (14sts)
- Work 5 rows SS starting with P
- 23rd row: K1, inc in next, K4, inc in next, inc in next, K4, inc in next, K1   (18sts)
- Work 11 rows SS starting with P
- 35th row: K1, sl1, K1, psso, K12, K2tog, K1   (16sts)
- 36th row: P1, P2tog, P10, P2tog, P1   (14sts)
- 37th row: K1, sl1, K1, psso, K8, K2tog, K1   (12sts)
- 38th row: P
- Cast off

To make up: Join front to back. Stuff.

ARMS

COLOUR I
- Size 10/3.25mm needles

WORKING FROM SHOULDER TO WRIST
- Cast on 5
- 1st row: K
- 2nd row: P
- 3rd row K1, inc in next, K1, inc in next, K1   (7sts)
- 4th row: P
- 5th row: K1, inc in next, K3, inc in next, K1   (9sts)

- 6th row: P
- 7th row: K3, inc in next, K1, inc in next, K3   (11sts)
- 8th row: P
- 9th row: K5, inc in next, K5   (12sts)
- Work 12 rows SS starting with P
- 22nd row: P2tog, P3, P2tog, P3, P2tog   (9sts)
- 23rd row: K2tog, K5, K2tog   (7sts)
- 24th row: P
- 25th row: K1 inc in next, K3, inc in next, K1   (9sts)
- 26th row: P
- 27th row: K3, inc in next, K1, inc in next, K3   (11sts)
- Work 3 rows SS starting with P
- 31st row: K1, Ktog, K5, K2tog, K1   (9sts)
- 32nd row: P
- 33rd row: K
- 34th row: P1, P2tog, P3, P2tog, P1   (7sts)
- 35th row: K
- 36th row: P
- 37th row: K1, K2tog, K1, K2tog, K1   (5sts)
- 38th row: P
- 39th row: K1, inc in next, K1, inc in next, K1   (7sts)
- 40th row: P
- 41st row: K1, inc in next, K3, inc in next, K1   (9sts)
- 42nd row: P

FOR LEFT HAND
- 43rd row: K2, put 2sts on pin, K5   (7sts)
- Work 4 rows SS starting with P
- 48th row: P2tog, P2tog, P2tog, P1   (4sts)
- 49th row: K2tog, K2tog   (2sts)
- Pull wool through

FOR RIGHT HAND
- 43rd row: K5, put 2sts on pin, K2 (7sts)
- Work 4 rows SS starting with P
- 48th row: P1, P2tog, P2tog, P2tog (4sts)
- 49th row: K2tog, K2tog (2sts)
- Pull wool through

THUMB – SAME FOR BOTH HANDS
- Join wool to 2sts on pin
- Use 2.75mm double-ended to work i-cord for 3 rows
- Pull wool through and darn end

To make up: Join seams. Stuff. Attach to body.

LEGS
COLOUR 2 – USE AS DOUBLE THREAD
- Size 11/3.00mm needles

- Cast on 24
- 1st row: K
- 2nd row: P
- 3rd row: K10, K2tog, K2tog, K10 (22sts)
- 4th row: P10, P2tog, P10 (21sts)
- 5th row: K5, (K2tog, K1)x3, K2tog, K5 (17sts)
- 6th row: P
- 7th row: K4, cast off 8, K4 (9sts)
- 8th row: P, pulling 2 sections tog
- Work 4 rows SS starting with K
- 13th row: K1, inc in next, K5, inc in next, K1 (11sts)
- Work 3 rows SS starting with P
- 17th row: K1, inc in next, K7, inc in next, K1 (13sts)
- Work 3 rows SS starting with P
- 21st row: K1, inc in next, K9, inc in

next, K1 (15sts)
- 22nd row: P
- 23rd row: K1, inc in next, K11, inc in next, K1 (17sts)
- Work 3 rows SS starting with P
- 27th row: K1, sl1, K1, psso, K11, K2tog, K1 (15sts)
- 28th row: P1, P2tog, P9, P2tog, P1 (13sts)
- 29th row: K1, sl1, K1, psso, K7, K2tog, K1 (11sts)
- Work 3 rows SS starting with P
- 33rd row: K1, inc in next, K7, inc in next, K1 (13sts)
- Work 3 rows SS starting with P
- 37th row: K1, inc in next, K9, inc in next, K1 (15sts)
- Work 3 rows SS starting with P
- 41st row: K1, inc in next, K11, inc in next, K1 (17sts)
- Work 3 rows SS starting with P
- 45th row: K1, inc in next, K13, inc in next, K1 (19sts)
- 46th row: P
- 47th row: K1, inc in next, K15, inc in next, K1 (21sts)
- Work 14 rows SS starting with P
- Cast off

To make up: Join seams. Stuff. Attach to body.

HEAD
COLOUR 1
- Size 10/3.25mm needles

HEAD – BACK
- Cast on 6
- 1st row: K
- 2nd row: P
- 3rd row: K1, inc in next, K2, inc in next, K1 (8sts)
- Work 3 rows SS starting with P
- 7th row: K1, inc in next, K4, inc in

next, K1 (10sts)
- 8th row: P
- 9th row: K3, inc in next, K2, inc in next, K3 (12sts)
- 10th row: P
- 11th row: K2, (inc in next)x3, K2, (inc in next)x3, K2 (18sts)
- Work 3 rows SS starting with P
- 15th row: K4, (inc in next, K2)x3, inc in next, K4 (22sts)
- Work 3 rows SS starting with P
- 19th row: K1, sl1, K1, psso, K2, (sl1, K1, psso)x2, K4, (K2tog)x2, K2, K2tog, K1 (16sts)
- 20th row: P
- 21st row: K1, (sl1, K1, psso)x3, (K2tog) x4, K1 (8sts)
- 2nd row: P
- Cast off

HEAD – FRONT (RIGHT SIDE)
- Cast on 5
- 1st row: K
- 2nd row: P
- 3rd row: Cast on 2, K to end (7sts)
- 4th row: P5, inc in next, inc in next (9sts)
- 5th row: K1, inc in next, inc in next, K6 (11sts)
- 6th row: P11 – break wool, leave sts on needle

HEAD – FRONT (LEFT SIDE)
- With WS facing cast on 5, turn – now working on these 5sts only:
- 1st row: K
- 2nd row: P
- 3rd row: K, cast on 2 (7sts)
- 4th row: P1, inc in next, inc in next, P4 (9sts)
- 5th row: K6, inc in next, inc in next, K1 (11sts)
- 6th row: P11
- 7th row: K across 2 pieces to join, K10,

- K2tog, K10 (21sts)
- 8th row: P1, P2tog, P15, P2tog, P1 (19sts)
- Work 6 rows SS starting with K
- 15th row: K1, sl1, K1, psso, K13, K2tog, K1 (17sts)
- 16th row: P
- 17th row: K1, sl1, K1, psso, K11, K2tog, K1 (15sts)
- 18th row: P
- 19th row: K1, sl1, K1, psso, K9, K2tog, K1 (13sts)
- 20th row: P1, P2tog, P7, P2tog, P1 (11sts)
- 21st row: K1, sl1, K1, psso, K5, K2tog, K1 (9sts)
- 22nd row: P
- Cast off

To make up: Join seam under chin. Join front and back tog. Stuff. Attach to body.

SHIRT

COLOUR 4
- Size 13/2.25mm needles

- Cast on 68
- Work 3 rows K
- 4th row: K2, P to last 2, K2
- 5th row: K
- Repeat rows 4 & 5 (x13)
- 32nd row: K2, P to last 2, K2
- 33rd row: K17, cast off 2, K29, cast off 2, K16 (64sts)
-

FRONT LEFT SIDE – WITH WS FACING
- Working on 17sts – Put remaining sts on pin
- Work 16 rows SS starting with P – Each P row starting with K2
- 17th row: Cast off 3, P to end (14sts)
- 18th row: K14

- 19th row: Cast off 2, P to end (12sts)
- 20th row: Cast off 5, K to end (7sts)
- 21st row: P
- 22nd row: Cast off 7
- Pull wool through

SHIRT – BACK
- Working on next 30sts from pin:
- Work 18 rows SS starting with P
- Cast off

FRONT RIGHT SIDE
- Working on remaining 17sts
- Work 15 rows SS starting with P – Each P row ending with K2
- 16th row: Cast off 3, K to end (14sts)
- 17th row: P all sts
- 18th row: Cast off 2, K to end (12sts)
- 19th row: Cast off 5, P to end (7sts)
- 20th row: K
- Cast off

SLEEVES – MAKE TWO
- Cast on 34
- Work 9 rows starting with K
- 10th row: P1, P2tog, P28, P2tog, P1 (32sts)
- Work 9 rows SS starting with K
- 20th row: P1, P2tog, P26, P2tog, P1 (30sts)
- Work 9 rows SS starting with K
- 30th row: P1, P2tog, P24, P2tog, P1 (28sts)
- Work 25 rows SS starting with K
- Cast off

To make up: Join shoulder and sleeve seams. Inset sleeves. Dress doll and lace front together with COLOUR 6. Roll up sleeves to just below elbow.

BREECHES

COLOUR 3
- Size 11/3.00mm needles
LEFT LEG
- Cast on 20
- 1st row: K
- 2nd row: P
- 3rd row: K1, inc in next, K16, inc in next, K1 (22sts)
- Work 3 rows SS starting with P
- 7th row: K1, inc in next, K18, inc in next, K1 (24sts)
- Work 5 rows SS starting with P
- 13th row: K1, inc in next, K20, inc in next, K1 (26sts)
- Work 5 rows SS starting with P
- 19th row: K1, inc in next, K22, inc in next, K1 (28sts)
- Work 9 rows SS starting with P
- 29th row: Cast off 2, K2, inc in next, K2, inc in next, K17, cast off last 2sts, pull wool through
- Leave remaining sts on needle

RIGHT LEG
- Cast on 20
- Repeat rows 1 to 28
- 29th row: Cast off 2, K17, inc in next, K2, inc in next, K5

TO JOIN THE LEGS TOGETHER
- 30th row: Cast off 2, P25 from right leg, using last st from right and 1st from left P2tog, P25 (51sts)
- 31st row: K1, sl1, K1, psso, K45, K2tog, K1 (49sts)
- Work 5 rows SS starting with P
- 37th row: K1, sl1, K1, psso, K43, K2tog, K1 (47sts)
- Work 6 rows SS starting with P
- Cast off

To make up: join inside leg seams. Join through crotch. Dress doll. Wind length of COLOUR 6 around waist of breeches twice and secure in place.

BINDINGS AT KNEES OF BREECHES

Work two 20cm crochet chains: one in COLOUR 2, one in COLOUR 6. Wind around the bottom of breeches to tighten to the legs at the narrowest point above the calf-shaping, and catch into place.

BLANKET

This is a crocheted item

Abbreviations: ch – chain
dc – double crochet
tr – treble crochet

COLOUR 5

- Size 2.50mm crochet hook
-

WORKING FROM SHOULDER TO HEM
BACK

- 1st row: make 37 ch
- 2nd row: work 34 dc starting in 3rd ch from hook, 2 ch, turn –
- 3rd row: 1 dc in next, (2 ch, miss next dc, work dc in next 2)x11, 2 ch, turn –
- 4th row: (2 dc into space, 2 ch)x11, 2 ch, 1 dc into end loop, 2 ch
- 5th row: 1 dc into space, 2 ch, (2 dc into space, 2 ch)x10, 1 dc into last loop, 2 ch
- Repeat row 5 (x2)
- 8th row: (2 dc into space, 2 ch)x10, miss last space, turn –
- 9th row: (2 dc into space, 2 ch)x9, miss last space, turn –
- 10th row: (2 dc into space, 2 ch)x8, miss last space, turn –
- 11th row: (2 dc into space, 2 ch)x8
- Repeat row 11 (x10)

- 22nd row: (2 dc into space, 2 ch)x7, miss last space, turn –
- 23rd row: (2 ch into space, 2 ch)x7
- Repeat row 23 (x3)
- 27th row: (2 dc into space, 2 ch)x6, miss last space, turn –
- 28th row: (2 dc into space, 2 ch)x5, miss last space, turn -–
- 29th row: (2 dc into space, 2 ch)x5
- 30th row: (2 dc into space, 2 ch)x4, miss last space, turn –
- 31st row: (2 dc into space, 2 ch)x3, miss last space, turn –
- 32nd row: (2 dc into space, 2 ch)x2, miss last space, turn –
- 33rd row: 2 dc into space, 2 ch, sl into last loop, pull wool through

TO CREATE RIGHT FRONT

- Go back to shoulder, join wool into 8th loop from right-hand edge
- 1st row: 3 dc, 3 tr, 2 ch, turn –
- 2nd row: 11 dc, 2 dc into last loop, 2 ch
- 3rd row: (dc in next 2 loops, 2 ch, miss 1 loop)x4, 2 dc into last loop, 2 ch
- 4th row: (2 dc into space, 2 ch)x5
- Repeat row 4 (x9)
- 14th row: (2 dc into space, 2 ch)x4, miss last space, turn –
- 15th row: (2 dc into space, 2 ch)x4
- Repeat row 15 (x10)
- 26th row: (2 dc into space, 2 ch)x3, miss last space, turn –
- 27th row: (2 dc into space, 2 ch)x3
- Repeat row 27 (x4)
- 32nd row: (2 dc into space, 2 ch)x2, miss last space, turn –
- 33rd row: (2 dc into space, 2 ch)x2
- 34th row: (2 dc into space, 2 ch)x1, miss last space, turn –
- 35th row: 2 dc, pull wool through

TO CREATE LEFT FRONT

- Turn work over and start on right-hand edge again, join wool into 8th ch from edge
- 1st row: 3 dc, 3 tr, 2 ch, turn –
- 2nd row: 11 dc, 2 dc into last loop, 2 ch
- 3rd row: (dc into next 2 loops, 2 ch, miss 1 loop)x4, 2 dc into last loop, 2 ch
- 4th row: (2 dc into space, 2 ch)x5
- 5th row: (2 dc into space, 2 ch)x5
- Repeat row 5 (x6)
- 12th row: (2 dc into space, 2 ch)x4, miss last space, turn –
- 13th row: (2 dc into space, 2 ch)x4
- Repeat row 13 (x6)
- 20th row: (2 dc into space, 2 ch)x3, miss last space, turn –
- 21st row: (2 dc into space, 2 ch)x3
- Repeat row 21 (x2)
- 24th row: (2 dc into space, 2 ch)x2, miss last space, turn –
- 25th row: (2dc into space, 2 ch)x2
- Repeat row 25 (x3)
- 29th row: 2 dc into space, 2 ch, miss last space, turn –
- 30th row: 2 dc into space, 2 ch
- Repeat row 30
- Pull wool through

To make up: Fold in half along the shoulder line and catch loosely under the arm. Add loops of wool to make fringing in a random fashion along the shaped edge. Dress doll. Catch at centre front to hold in place ready for belt to be placed over the top.

CAPE

COLOUR 6

- Size 12/2.75mm needles

- Cast on 36
- 1st row: K
- 2nd row: K1, P to last, K1
- 3rd row: K3, (inc in next, K1)x15, K3
- 4th row: K1, P to last, K1
- 5th row: K
- 6th row: K1, P to last, K1
- 7th row: K4, (inc in next, K2)x14, inc in next, K4 (66sts)
- 8th row: K1, P to last, K1
- 9th row: K
- 10th row: K1, P to last, K1
- 11th row: K4, (inc in next, K2)x19, inc in next, K4 (86sts)
- 12th row: K1, P to last, K1
- 13th row: K
- Repeat rows 12 & 13 (x3)
- Cast off

HOOD

COLOUR 6

- Size 12/2.75mm needles

- Cast on 18
- 1st row: K
- 2nd row: P
- 3rd row: K
- 4th row: P
- 5th row: K16, inc in next, K1 (19sts)
- 6th row: P
- 7th row: K17, inc in next, K1 (20sts)
- 8th row: P
- 9th row: K
- 10th row: P
- 11th row: K18, inc in next, K1 (21sts)
- 12th row: P
- 13th row: K19, inc in next, K1 (22sts)
- 14th row: P
- 15th row: K20, inc in next, K1 (23sts)
- 16th row: P
- 17th row: K21, inc in next, K1 (24sts)
- 18th row: P
- 19th row: K22, inc in next, K1 (25sts)
- 20th row: P
- 21st row: K23, inc in next, K1 (26sts)
- 22nd row: P
- 23rd row: K
- 24th row: P
- 25th row: K24, inc in next, K1 (27sts)
- 26th row: P
- 27th row: K
- 28th row: P
- 29th row: K25, inc in next, K1 (28sts)
- 30th row: P
- 31st row: K
- 32nd row: P
- 33rd row: K17, turn –
- 34th row: sl1, P15, K1
- 35th row: K
- 36th row: P
- 37th row: K17, turn –
- 38th row: sl1, P15, K1
- 39th row: K
- 40th row: P
- 41st row: K25, K2tog, K1 (27sts)
- 42nd row: P
- 43rd row: K
- 44th row: P
- 45th row: K24, K2tog, K1 (26sts)
- 46th row: P
- 47th row: K
- 48th row: P
- 49th row: K23, K2tog, K1 (25sts)
- 50th row: P
- 51st row: K22, K2tog, K1 (24sts)
- 52nd row: P
- 53rd row: K21, K2tog, K1 (23sts)
- 54th row: P
- 55th row: K20, K2tog, K1 (22sts)
- 56th row: P
- 57th row: K19, K2tog, K1 (21sts)
- 58th row: P
- 59th row: K18, K2tog, K1 (20sts)
- 60th row: P
- 61st row: K
- 62nd row: P
- 63rd row: K17, K2tog, K1 (19sts)
- 64th row: P
- 65th row: K16, K2tog, K1 (18sts)
- 66th row: P
- 67th row: K
- 68th row: P
- 69th row: K
- Cast off

To make up: The straight edge is the front of the hood. Fold in half and sew-up shaped edge. Sew cast on and cast off edges to the curved neck of the cape. Dress doll. Make crochet chain ties at front neck of cape. Hold in place with catch-stitches.

SWORD BELT

COLOUR 7

- Size 12/2.75mm needles

- Cast on 3
- Work GS until the belt measures 26cm. Make buckle from gold wire, attach and sew belt together around waist. Crochet approx. 4cm of chain to make a loop for the belt on which to hang the sword.

QUIVER

COLOUR 7

- Size 12/2.75mm needles

- Cast on 4
- Work in GS
- 1st row: K
- 2nd row: Inc in every st (8sts)
- Work 4 rows GS
- 7th row: K1, inc in next, K3, inc in next, K2 (10sts)

- Work 12 rows GS
- 20th row: K2, inc in next, K4, inc in next, K2 (12sts)
- Work 18 rows GS
- Cast off

To make up: Sew into a cone shape and sew bottom end to sword belt at centre back. Crochet chain from top edge of Quiver long enough to thread over shoulder to join sword belt at front right side. Stitch in place.

BOOTS

COLOUR 6
- Size 11/3.00mm needles

RIGHT BOOT
- Cast on 32
- 1st row: K
- 2nd row: P
- 3rd row: K9, K2tog, K2tog, K19 (30sts)
- 4th row: P19, P2tog, P9   (29sts)
- 5th row: K4, (K2tog, K1)x3, K2tog, K14 (25sts)
- 6th row: P
- 7th row: K19, K2tog, K4
- 8th row: K1, P8, cast off 13, K1   (11sts)
- 9th row: K11 pulling sections tog
- Work 5 rows SS starting with P – On all P rows knit 1st & last st
- 15th row: K5, inc in next, K1, inc in next, K3 (13sts)
- 16th row: K1, P to last, K1
- 17th row: K6, inc in next, K1, inc in next, K4 (15sts)
- 18th row: K1, P to last, K1
- 19th row: K7, inc in next, K1, inc in next, K5 (17sts)
- Work 3 rows SS starting with P– On all P rows knit 1st & last st
- 23rd row: K8, inc in next, K1, inc in next, K6 (19sts)

- Work 6 rows SS starting with K – On all P rows knit 1st & last st
- Cast off

LEFT BOOT
- Cast on 32
- 1st row: K
- 2nd row: P
- 3rd row: K19, K2tog, K2tog, K9 (30sts)
- 4th row: P9, K2tog, P19   (29sts)
- 5th row: K14, (K2tog, K1)x3, K2tog, K4   (25sts)
- 6th row: P
- 7th row: K4, K2tog, K19   (24sts)
- 8th row: K1, cast off 13, P8, K1   (11sts)
- 9th row: K11 pulling sections together
- Work 5 rows SS starting with P – On all P rows knit 1st & last st
- 15th row: K3, inc in next, K1, inc in next, K5 (13sts)
- 16th row: K1, P to last, K1
- 17th row: K4, inc in next, K1, inc in next, K6 (15sts)
- 18th row: K1, P to last, K1
- 19th row: K5, inc in next, K1, inc in next, K7 (17sts)
- Work 3 rows SS starting with P – On all P rows knit 1st & last st
- 23rd row: K6, inc in next, K1, inc in next, K8 (19sts)
- Work 6 rows SS starting with K – On all P rows knit 1st & last st
- Cast off

To make up: Join instep seam as far as ankle. Join along the top of the foot. Join under the foot to make boot shape. Fold the cuff over and stab through to hold in place. Put onto feet and lace loosely up the inside leg.

SWORD

Cut shaped piece of boning for blade and cross-hilt. Join using craft wire. Paint and decorate with Hot-fix studs, wire and fine gold cord.

BOW & ARROW

To make 4 arrows, use kebab skewers or similar and cut to approx. 14cm. File down sharp ends. For the feathers use 3 lozenge shape pieces of interfacing, approx. 3.5cm long, per arrow. Fold in half lengthwise and glue to shaft of skewer. Trim to feather-shape. Bind fine twine around base of feather for effect. Glue in place.

To make bow we used a small piece of cane, but a curved twig from the garden or something similar would work equally well. Create string of bow with fine twine and add detail of the hand grip. Glue in place.

HAIR

Cut lengths of charcoal black fine wool and black silk embroidery thread and knot in using 2.00mm crochet hook. Work from front to back of head, using a small quantity at a time. The lengths should be slightly longer than the finished length. Once head of hair is complete use hairdressing scissors to layer hair to shape.

FEATURES

Eyebrows are worked in the same yarn as for the hair. Add mouth in appropriate colour. Add brown beads for eyes. Nose and ears are crochet chains stitched in place.

You will need

MATERIALS:

Colour Codes:

1 Rowan Baby Merino Silk DK (Shade SH674 – Shell Pink) – For Body

2 Sirdar Calico DK (Shade 0723 – White) – For Legs

3 Debbie Bliss Andes (Shade 370019 – Pale Grey) – For Doublet & Garters

4 Wendy Supreme Cotton DK (Shade 1945 – Pale Grey) – For Shoes

5 Rowan Panama (Shade 00306 – Rust Red) – For Over-Robe

6. Gedifra Aneja (Shade 01121 – Copper) – For Trim of Over-Robe

7 Rowan Kidsilk Haze (Shade 00649 – Rust) – For Hair & Beard

8 Rowan Kidsilk Haze (Shade 00658 – Gold) – For Trim of Over-Robe. Use together with No.9 as double thread

9 Rowan Fine Lace (Shade 00930 – Gold) Use together with No.8 as double thread

10 Rowan Lima (Shade 895 – Dark Brown) – For Fur Collar

11 SMC Extra Soft Merino (Shade 05114 – Black) – For Hat

Feathers for hat trim
Beads/lace/old jewellery
Small piece of plastic boning
for codpiece
Stuffing

NEEDLES:

Size 9/3.75mm
Size 10/3.25mm
Size 10/3.25mm double-ended
Size 11/3.00mm
Crochet hook 2.50mm
Darning needle

Henry VIII

The reign of Henry VIII was one of the most eventful in our nation's history. King at eighteen years of age, he would rule for nearly forty years, a reign full of political intrigue, religious battles with Rome, war and, of course, a very complex and bloody personal life. Henry started off his reign by having two of his father Henry VII's least popular advisers executed. He then married Catherine of Aragon, cementing a bond with mighty Spain, but Catherine's failure to produce a male heir left Henry with a serious dilemma. His attempts to annul the marriage, against the papal will, started the English Reformation and centuries of religious upheaval. He then married Anne Boleyn but the unlucky Anne was executed after also failing to give birth to a boy. Jane Seymour followed, then Anne of Cleves, Catherine Howard and Catherine Parr. Only Jane could produce an heir, Edward VI, that survived for more than a short time but sadly he died aged fifteen, and Catherine Howard met a grisly end after her affair with Thomas Culpeper.

As well as his battles on the personal front, Henry VIII had the French, the Spanish and the Scots to contend with. He also had Thomas Cromwell in his employ, a man who had a driving ambition to sort out the country's finances and to promote the Reformation, brought to life most recently in *Wolf Hall* by Hilary Mantel. Cromwell had his work cut out because, although Henry VIII had inherited a huge sum of money from his father, he spent lavishly and well beyond his means, bringing the country perilously close to bankruptcy.

Our splendidly attired Henry VIII is based on the classic portrait by Hans Holbein the Younger, and shows a king in all his pomp, a man who ruled absolutely and did pretty much exactly as he pleased.

BODY

COLOUR 1
- Size 10/3.25mm needles

BODY – FRONT
- Cast on 16
- 1st row: K
- 2nd row: P
- 3rd row: K1, inc in next, K12, inc in next, K1   (18sts)
- 4th row: P
- 5th row: K
- 6th row: P
- 7th row: K1, K2tog, K12, K2tog, K1   (16sts)
- 8th row: P
- 9th row: K
- 10th row: P
- 11th row: K5, inc in next, K4, inc in next, K5   (18sts)
- 12th row: P13, turn –
- 13th row: K4, inc in next, K3, turn –
- 14th row: P14
- 15th row: K9, inc in next, K9   (20sts)
- 16th row: P16, turn –
- 17th row: K5, inc in next, inc in next, K5, turn –
- 18th row: P18
- 19th row: K to end
- 20th row: P
- 21st row: K
- 22nd row: P
- 23rd row: K1, inc in next, K18, inc in next, K1   (24sts)
- 24th row: P
- 25th row: K
- 26th row: P
- 27th row: K4, K2tog, K12, K2tog, K4   (22sts)
- 28th row: P
- 29th row: K
- 30th row: P
- 31st row: K
- 32nd row: P10, P2tog, P10   (21sts)

- 33rd row: K1, sl1, K1, psso, K15, K2tog, K1   (19sts)
- 34th row: P1, P2tog, P13, P2tog, P1   (17sts)
- 35th row: K1, sl1, K1, psso, K11, K2tog, K1   (15sts)
- 36th row: P
- Cast off

BODY – BACK
- Cast on 16
- 1st row: K
- 2nd row: P
- 3rd row: K2, inc in next, K1, inc in next, K6, inc in next, K1, inc in next, K2   (20sts)
- 4th row: P
- 5th row: K3, inc in next, K1, inc in next, K8, inc in next, K1, inc in next, K3   (24sts)
- Work 5 rows SS starting with P
- 11th row: K1, K2tog, K18, K2tog, K1   (22sts)
- 12th row: P
- 13th row: K2, K2tog, K2, K2tog, K6, K2tog, K2, K2tog, K2   (18sts)
- 14th row: P
- 15th row: (K2, K2tog)x4, K2   (14sts)
- Work 5 rows SS starting with P
- 21st row: K1, inc in next, K4, inc in next, inc in next, K4, inc in next, K1   (18sts)
- 22nd row: P
- 23rd row: K1, inc in next, K14, inc in next, K1   (20sts)
- Work 9 rows SS starting with P
- 33rd row: K1, sl1, K1, psso, K14, K2tog, K1   (18sts)
- 34th row: P1, P2tog, P12, P2tog, P1   (16sts)
- 35th row: K1, sl1, K1, psso, K10, K2tog, K1   (14sts)
- 36th row: P
- Cast off

To make up: Join back to front. Stuff.

ARMS – MAKE TWO

COLOUR 1
- Size 10/3.25mm needles

- WORKING FROM SHOULDER TO WRIST
- Cast on 5
- 1st row: K
- 2nd row: P
- 3rd row: K1, inc in next, K1, inc in next, K1   (7sts)
- 4th row: P
- 5th row: K1, inc in next, K3, inc in next, K1   (9sts)
- Work 27 rows SS starting with P

FOR LEFT HAND:
- 33rd row: K2, put next 2sts on pin, K5
- 34th row: P to end pulling sections together   (7sts)
- Work 3 rows SS starting with K
- 38th row: P2tog, P2tog, P2tog, P1   (4sts)
- 39th row: K2tog, K2tog   (2sts)
- Pull wool through

FOR RIGHT HAND:
- 33rd row: K5, put next 2sts on pin, K2   (7sts)
- 34th row: P to end pulling sections tog   (7sts)
- Work 3 rows SS starting with K
- 38th row: P1, P2tog, P2tog, P2tog   (4sts)
- 39th row: K2tog, K2tog   (2sts)
- Pull wool through

THUMBS
- Both the same – on double-ended needles work 2sts i-cord for 2 rows
- 3rd row: K2tog
- Pull wool through

To make up: Join seams. Stuff. Attach to body.

LEGS WITH SHOES ATTACHED – MAKE TWO

COLOUR 4

- Size 11/3.00mm needles

- Cast on 14
- Work 7 rows SS starting with K
- 8th row: P1, P2tog, P8, P2tog, P1 (12sts)
- 9th row: K1, K2tog, K6, K2tog, K1 (10sts)
- 10th row: P
- 11th row: K1, inc in next, K2, turn –
- 12th row: P2tog, P3 (4sts)
- Work 5 rows SS starting with K on these 4sts
- Cast off

- Put 2sts on pin – work on 4sts
- 11th row: K2, inc in next (5sts)
- 12th row: P3, P2tog (4sts)
- Work 5 rows SS starting with K
- Cast off

CHANGE TO COLOUR 2

- 1st row: Pick up 5sts from right-hand end – K2 from pin, pick up 5sts from left-hand end (12sts)
- 2nd row: P
- 3rd row: K
- 4th row: P2, P2tog, P4, P2tog, P2 (10sts)
- 5th row: K
- 6th row: P2, P2tog, P2, P2tog, P2 (8sts)
- 7th row: K
- 8th row: P
- 9th row: K
- 10th row: P
- 11th row: K1, inc in next, K4, inc in next, K1 (10sts)

- 12th row: P
- 13th row: K
- 14th row: P
- 15th row: K1, inc in next, K6, inc in next, K1 (12sts)
- 16th row: P
- 17th row: K
- 18th row: P
- 19th row: K1, inc in next, K8, inc in next, K1 (14sts)
- 20th row: P
- 21st row: K1, inc in next, K10, inc in next, K1 (16sts)
- 22nd row: P
- 23rd row: K
- 24th row: P
- 25th row: K1, sl1, K1, psso, K10, K2tog, K1 (14sts)
- 26th row: P1, P2tog, P8, P2tog, P1 (12sts)
- 27th row: K1, sl1, K1, psso, K6, K2tog, K1 (10sts)
- 28th row: P
- 29th row: K
- 30th row: P
- 31st row: K1, inc in next, K6, inc in next, K1 (12sts)
- 32nd row: P
- 33rd row: K
- 34th row: P
- 35th row: K1, inc in next, K8, inc in next, K1 (14sts)
- 36th row: P
- 37th row: K
- 38th row: P
- 39th row: K1, inc in next, K10, inc in next, K1 (16sts)
- 40th row: P
- 41st row: K
- 42nd row: P
- 43rd row: K1, inc in next, K12, inc in next, K1 (18sts)
- 44th row: P
- 45th row: K1, inc in next, K14, inc in next, K1 (20sts)

- Work 13 rows SS starting with P
- Cast off

To make up: Join leg seams. Stuff. Attach to body.

HEAD

COLOUR 1

- Size 10/3.25mm needles

HEAD – FRONT

- Cast on 6
- 1st row: K
- 2nd row: P
- 3rd row: K
- 4th row: P
- 5th row: K1, inc in next, K2, inc in next, K1 (8sts)
- 6th row: P3, inc in next, inc in next, P3 (10sts)
- 7th row: K3, (inc in next)x4, K3 (14sts)
- 8th row: P
- 9th row: K3, inc in next, K6, inc in next, K3 (16sts)
- 10th row: P3, inc in next, P8, inc in next, P3 (18sts)
- Work 5 rows SS starting with K
- 16th row: P1, P2tog, P12, P2tog, P1 (16sts)
- Work 4 rows SS starting with K
- 21st row: K1, sl1, K1, psso, K10, K2tog, K1 (14sts)
- 22nd row: P
- 23rd row: K1, sl1, K1, psso, K8, K2tog, K1 (12sts)
- 24th row: P1, P2tog, P6, P2tog, P1 (10sts)
- Cast off

HEAD – BACK

- Cast on 6
- 1st row: K
- 2nd row: P

- 3rd row: K1, inc in next, K2, inc in next, K1 (8sts)
- 4th row: P
- 5th row: K1, inc in next, K4, inc in next, K1 (10sts)
- 6th row: P
- 7th row: K1, inc in next, K1, inc in next, K2, inc in next, K1, inc in next, K1 (14sts)
- 8th row: P1, inc in next, P10, inc in next, P1 (16sts)
- 9th row: K1, inc in next, K1, inc in next, (K2, inc in next)×3, K1, inc in next, K1 (22sts)
- Work 3 rows SS starting with P
- 13th row: K6, inc in next, (K2, inc in next)×3, K6 (26sts)
- Work 7 rows SS starting with P
- 21st row: K1, sl1, K1, psso, K4, K2tog, K2tog, K4, K2tog, K2tog, K4, K2tog, K1 (20sts)
- 22nd row: P
- 23rd row: K1, sl1, K1, psso, (K2tog)×8, K1 (11sts)
- 24th row: P1, P2tog, P5, P2tog, P1 (9sts)
- Cast off

To make up: Join two pieces together. Stuff. Attach to body.

DOUBLET

COLOUR 3
- Size 10/3.25mm needles

- Cast on 34
- 1st row: K25, turn –
- 2nd row: P16, turn –
- 3rd row: K6, inc in next, K2, inc in next, K15 (36sts)
- 4th row: P26, turn –
- 5th row: K6, inc in next, K2, inc in next, K6, turn – (38sts)
- 6th row: P6, inc in next, P4, inc in

next, P16 (40sts)
- 7th row: K
- 8th row: P
- 9th row: K1, inc in next, K5, inc in next, K24, inc in next, K5, inc in next, K1 (44sts)
- 10th row: P
- 11th row: K9, inc in next, K2, inc in next, K18, inc in next, K2 inc in next, K9 (48sts)
- Work 3 rows SS starting with P
- 15th row: K16, sl1, K1, psso, K12, K2tog, K16 (46sts)
- 16th row: P

AT START OF ARMHOLES – WORKING ON LEFT BACK ON 12STS:
- 17th row: K12, turn –
- Work 4 rows SS starting with P
- 22nd row: P4, P2tog, P6 (11sts)
- 23rd row: K
- 24th row: P3, P2tog, P6 (10sts)
- 25th row: K
- 26th row: P
- Cast off

WORKING ON FRONT ON 22STS:
- Work 3 rows SS starting with K
- 20th row: P10, P2tog, P10 (21sts)
- 21st row: K
- 22nd row: P4, P2tog, P9, P2tog, P4 (19sts)
- 23rd row: K
- 24th row: P3, P2tog, P9, P2tog, P3 (17sts)
- Work 4 rows SS starting with K
- Cast off

WORKING ON RIGHT BACK ON 12STS:
- Work 5 rows SS starting with K
- 22nd row: P6, P2tog, P4 (11sts)

- 23rd row: K
- 24th row: P6, P2tog, P3 (10sts)
- 25th row: K
- 26th row: P
- Cast off

SLEEVES – MAKE TWO

COLOUR 3
- Size 10/3.25mm needles

- Cast on 12
- Work 6 rows SS starting with K
- 7th row: K1, inc in next, K8, inc in next, K1 (14sts)
- Work 7 rows SS starting with P
- 15th row: K1, inc in next, K10, inc in next, K1 (16sts)
- Work 8 rows SS starting with P
- 24th row: Cast off 3, P to end (13sts)
- 25th row: Cast off 3, K to end (10sts)
- 26th row: P
- Cast off

SKIRT

COLOUR 3
- Size 10/3.25mm needles

RIGHT-HAND SIDE, RS FACING:
- Cast on 108
- 1st row: P2, (K9, P3)×8, K9, P1
- 2nd row: K1, (P9, K3)×8, P9, K2
- Repeat rows 1 & 2 twice
- 7th row: P2, (K4, K2tog, K3, P3)×8, K4, K2tog, K3, P1 (99sts)
- 8th row: K1, (P8, K3)×8, P8, K2
- 9th row: P2, (K8, P3)×8, K8, P1
- 10th row: K1, (P8, K3)×8, P8, K2
- 11th row: P2, (K3, K2tog, K3, P3)×8, K3, K2tog, K3, P1 (90sts)
- 12th row: K1, (P7, K3)×8, P7, K2
- 13th row: P2, (K7, P3)×8, K7, P1
- 14th row: K1, (P7, K3)×8, P7, K2
- 15th row: P2, (K3, sl1, K1, psso, K2, P3)

- x8, K3, sll, K1, psso, K2, P1   (81sts)
- 16th row: K1, (P6, K3)x8, P6, K2
- 17th row: P2, (K6, P3)x8, K6, P1
- 18th row: K1, (P6, K3)x8, P6, K2
- 19th row: P2, (K2, sll, K1, psso, K2, P3)
  x8, K2, sll, K1, psso, K1, P1   (72sts)
- 20th row: K1, (P5, K3)x8, P5, K2
- 21st row: P2, (K5, P3)x8, K5, P1
- 22nd row: K1, (P1, P2tog, P2, K3)x8,
  P1, P2tog, P2, K2   (63sts)
- 23rd row: P2, (K4, P3)x8, K4, P1
- 24th row: K1, (P2tog, P2tog, K1,
  K2tog)x8, P2tog, P2tog, K2tog
  (36sts)
- 25th row: P1, (K2, P2)x8, K2, P1
- 26th row: K1, (P2, K2tog)x8, P2, K1
  (28sts)
- Cast off

LEFT-HAND SIDE, RS FACING:

- Cast on 108
- 1st row: P1, (K9, P3)x8, K9, P2
- 2nd row: K2, (P9, K3)x8, P9, K1
- Repeat rows 1 & 2 twice
- 7th row: P1, (K4, K2tog, K3, P3)x8, K4,
  K2tog, K3, P2   (99sts)
- 8th row: K2, (P8, K3)x8, P8, K1
- 9th row: P1, (K8, P3)x8, K8, P2
- 10th row: K2, (P8, K3)x8, P8, K1
- 11th row: P1, (K3, K2tog, K3, P3)x8,
  K3, K2tog, K3, P2   (90sts)
- 12th row: K2, (P7, K3)x8, P7, K1
- 13th row: P1, (K7, P3)x8, K7, P2
- 14th row: K2, (P7, K3)x8, P7, K1
- 15th row: P1, (K3, sll, K1, psso, K2, P3)
  x8, K3, sll, K1, psso, K2, P2   (81sts)
- 16th row: K2, (P6, K3)x8, P6, K1
- 17th row: P1, (K6, P3)x8, K6, P2
- 18th row: K2, (P6, K3)x8, P6, K1
- 19th row: P1, (K2, sll, K1, psso, K2, P3)
  x8, K2, sll, K1, psso, K1, P2   (72sts)
- 20th row: K2, (P5, K3)x8, P5, K1
- 21st row: P1, (K5, P3)x8, K5, P2
- 22nd row: K2, (P1, P2tog, P2, K3)x8,

P1, P2tog, P2, K1   (63sts)
- 23rd row: P1, (K4, P3)x8, K4, P2
- 24th row: K2tog, (P2tog, P2tog, K1,
  K2tog)x8, P2tog, P2tog, K1   (36sts)
- 25th row: P1, (K2, P2)x8, K2, P1
- 26th row: K1, (P2, K2tog)x8, P2, K1
  (28sts)
- Cast off

TO MAKE WHITE PUFFS ON SLEEVES & DOUBLET FRONT

Work 'clumps' of 2 or 3 buttonhole stitches in COLOUR 2, in vertical lines across the bodice and sleeves – use photo as reference. Sew small beads between these 'clumps' on the sleeves. Sew small beads at centre-front of doublet.

To make up: Join sleeve seams. Join shoulder seams. Insert sleeves. Join centre front of skirt at waist and attach to doublet.

*Tip: To control the folds of the skirt, run retaining threads on the wrong side.

CUFFS & RUFF AT NECK

Using COLOUR 2, crochet around cuffs and neck: one row of double crochet, and one row of 3-chain loops.

Dress doll with doublet & skirt – sew-up centre-back seam.

CODPIECE
COLOUR 3
- Size 11/3.00mm needles

- Cast on 5
- Work 14 rows SS starting with K
- 15th row: K2, inc in next, K2   (6sts)
- 16th row: P
- 17th row: K2, inc in next, inc in next,
  K2   (8sts)
- 18th row: P
- 19th row: K3, inc in next, inc in next,
  K3   (10sts)
- Work 12 rows SS starting with P
- 32nd row: P3, P2tog, P2tog, P3   (8sts)
- 33rd row: K
- 34th row: P2, P2tog, P2tog, P2   (6sts)
- 35th row: K
- 36th row: P2, P2tog, P2   (5sts)
- Work 14 rows SS starting with K
- Cast off

To make up: Fold 10cm-length of plastic boning in half. Sellotape ends together. Cover with codpiece, stitching sides together to completely cover the boning. Sew between legs of doll. Finish stitching centre-front seam of skirt around the codpiece.

GARTERS WITH ROSETTES

Using COLOUR 3, wind 4 threads around legs above calves and catch in place.
Make 2 rosettes: crochet 4-chain and make into circle. Work 4-chain and catch into loop four times. Pull wool through. Sew onto outside legs.

TIE BELT
COLOUR 2
- Crochet hook 2.50mm

- Work a 50cm chain. Wind around waist twice; tie in knot. Make loops in ends. Stitch in place.

OVER-ROBE

COLOUR 5
- Size 11/3.00mm needles

BACK YOKE
- Cast on 21
- Work 10 rows GS
- Cast off

FRONT OVER-ROBE – MAKE TWO
- SHOULDER TO HEM
- Cast on 6
- Work 6 rows SS starting with K
- 7th row: K2, inc in next, inc in next, K2   (8sts)
- Work 5 rows SS starting with P
- 13th row: K1, inc in next, K1, inc in next, inc in next, K1, inc in next, K1 (12sts)
- Work 7 rows SS starting with P
- 21st row: K1, (inc in next, K2)x3, inc in next, K1   (16sts)
- Work 7 rows SS starting with P
- 29th row: (K1, inc in next, K2, inc in next)x3, K1   (22sts)
- Work 7 rows SS starting with P
- 37th row: K1, (inc in next, K2)x3, inc in next, inc in next, (K2, inc in next)x3, K1   (30sts)
- Work 7 rows SS starting with P
- 45th row: K1, (inc in next, K2)x9, inc in next, K1   (40sts)
- Work 7 rows SS starting with P
- 53rd row: K2, (inc in next, K3)x4, inc in next, K2, (inc in next, K3)x4, inc in next, K2   (50sts)
- Work 7 rows SS starting with P
- 61st row: (K3, inc in next)x6, K2, (inc in next, K3)x6   (62sts)
- Put onto pin

BACK OVER-ROBE
- Work from under yoke to hem
- Cast on 66
- 1st row: K
- 2nd row: P
- 3rd row: K1, inc in next, K1, inc in next, inc in next, K1, inc in next, K52, inc in next, K1, inc in next, inc in next, K1, inc in next, K1   (74sts)
- Work 7 rows SS starting with P
- 11th row: K1, (inc in next, K2)x3, inc in next, K52, (inc in next, K2)x3, inc in next, K1   (82sts)
- Work 7 rows SS starting with P
- 19th row: (K1, inc in next, K2, inc in next)x3, K52, (inc in next, K2, inc in next, K1)x3   (94sts)
- Work 7 rows SS starting with P
- 27th row: K1, (inc in next, K2)x3, inc in next, (inc in next, K2)x3, inc in next, K52, inc in next, (K2, inc in next)x3, inc in next, (K2, inc in next)x3, K1   (110sts)
- Work 7 rows SS starting with P
- 35th row: K1, (inc in next, K2)x9, inc in next, K52, inc in next, (K2, inc in next)x9, K1   (130sts)
- Work 7 rows SS starting with P
- 43rd row: K2, (inc in next, K3)x4, inc in next, K2, (inc in next, K3)x4, inc in next, K54, inc in next, (K3, inc in next)x4, K2, inc in next, (K3, inc in next)x4, K2   (150sts)
- Work 7 rows SS starting with P
- 51st row: (K3, inc in next)x6, K2, (inc in next, K3)x6, K50, (K3, inc in next)x6, K2, (inc in next, K3)x6   (174sts)
- Leave stitches on needle

Pleat the cast-on edge to fit the long edge of yoke and sew in place.
Sew side seams from the bottom to within 4cm of the shoulder – this forms the armhole for the sleeve.

Now work on all the stitches along the hem edge: 62sts from right front, 174sts from back, 62sts from left front   (298sts)

- CHANGE TO COLOURS 8 & 9 – USED TOGETHER
- 1st row: P
- 2nd row: P
- CHANGE TO COLOUR 6
- Work 5 rows SS starting with P
- CHANGE TO COLOURS 8 & 9
- 8th row: K
- 9th row: K
- Cast off

To make up: Steam-press the pleats in place. Join shoulder seams.

OVER-ROBE SLEEVES – MAKE TWO

COLOURS 8 & 9
- Size 11/3.00mm needles

- Cast on 16
- 1st row: K
- 2nd row: K
- CHANGE TO COLOUR 6
- 3rd row: K
- 4th row: K1, P14, K1
- 5th row: K
- 6th row: K1, P14, K1
- 7th row: K14, inc in next, K1   (17sts)
- 8th row: K1, P15, K1
- CHANGE TO COLOURS 8 & 9
- 9th row: K
- 10th row: K
- CHANGE TO COLOUR 5
- 11th row: K15, inc in next, K1   (18sts)
- 12th row: K1, P16, K1
- 13th row: K
- 14th row: K1, P16, K1
- Repeat rows 13 & 14 (x2)
- 19th row: K16, inc in next, K1   (19sts)
- 20th row: K1, P17, K1

- 21st row: K9, K2tog, K8   (18sts)
- 22nd row: K1, P16, K1
- 23rd row: K
- 24th row: K1, P16, K1
- 25th row: K9, K2tog, K7   (17sts)
- 26th row: K1, P15, K1
- 27th row: K3, K2tog, K7, K2tog, K1, inc in next, K1   (16sts)
- 28th row: K1, P14, K1
- 29th row: K7, K2tog, K7
- 30th row: K1, P13, K1
- 31st row: K1, K2tog, K7, K2tog, K3 (13sts)
- 32nd row: K1, P6, P2tog, P3, K1 (12sts)
- 33rd row: K
- 34th row: K1, P10, K1   (12sts)
- 35th row: K4, K2tog, K6   (11sts)
- 36th row: K1, P9, K1 – Mark this row with a tag
- 37th row: K1, inc in next, K9   (12sts)
- 38th row: K1, P10, K1
- 39th row: K3, (inc in next, K1)x3, inc in next, K2   (16sts)
- 40th row: K1, P14, K1
- 41st row: K6, inc in next, K4, inc in next, K4   (18sts)
- 42nd row: K1, P16, K1
- 43rd row: K8, inc in next, K9   (19sts)
- 44th row: K1, P17, K1
- 45th row: K8, inc in next, K10   (20sts)
- 46th row: K1, P18, K1
- 47th row: K17, turn –
- 48th row: P14, turn –
- 49th row: K11, turn –
- 50th row: P11, turn –
- 51st row: K17
- 52nd row: K1, P18, K1   (20sts)
- CHANGE TO COLOURS 8 & 9
- 53rd row: K
- 54th row: K
- CHANGE TO COLOUR 6
- 55th row: K
- 56th row: K1, P18, K1

- 57th row: K
- 58th row: K1, P18, K1
- CHANGE TO COLOURS 8 & 9
- 59th row: K
- 60th row: K
- CHANGE TO COLOUR 5
- 61st row: K
- 62nd row: K1, P18, K1   (20sts)
- 63rd row: K3, (inc in next, K1)x7, K3 (27sts)
- 64th row: K1, P23, turn –
- 65th row: K21, turn –
- 66th row: P18, turn –
- 67th row: K3, inc in next, K7, inc in next, K3, turn –
- 68th row: P20, turn –
- 69th row: K11, inc in next, K11, turn –
- 70th row: P26, K1
- 71st row: K   (30sts) – Mark this row as shoulder
- 72nd row: K1, P26, turn –
- 73rd row: K11, K2tog, K11, turn –
- 74th row: P20, turn –
- 75th row: K3, K2tog, K7, K2tog, K3, turn –
- 76th row: P18, turn –
- 77th row: K21, turn –
- 78th row: P23, K1
- 79th row: K3, (K2tog, K1)x7, K3 (20sts)
- 80th row: K1, P18, K1
- CHANGE TO COLOURS 8 & 9
- 81st row: K
- 82nd row: K
- CHANGE TO COLOUR 6
- 83rd row: K
- 84th row: K1, P18, K1
- 85th row: K
- 86th row: K1, P18, K1
- CHANGE TO COLOURS 8 & 9
- 87th row: K
- 88th row: K
- CHANGE TO COLOUR 5
- 89th row: K

- 90th row: K1, P18, K1
- 91st row: K17, turn –
- 92nd row: P14, turn –
- 93rd row: K11, turn –
- 94th row: P11, turn –
- 95th row: K17
- 96th row: K1, P18, K1   (20sts)
- 97th row: K8, K2tog, K10   (19sts)
- 98th row: K1, P17, K1
- 99th row: K8, K2tog, K9
- 100th row: K1, P16, K1
- 101st row: K6, K2tog, K4, K2tog, K4 (16sts)
- 102nd row: K1, P14, K1
- 103rd row: K3, (K2tog, K1)x3, K2tog, K2   (12sts)
- 104th row: K1, P10, K1   (12sts)
- 105th row: K1, K2tog, K9   (11sts) – Mark this row with a tag
- 106th row: K1, P9, K1
- 107th row: K4, inc in next, K6   (12sts)
- 108th row: K1, P10, K1
- 109th row: K
- 110th row: K1, P6, inc in next, P3, K1 (13sts)
- 111th row: K1, inc in next, K7, inc in next, K3   (15sts)
- 112th row: K1, P13, K1
- 113th row: K7, inc in next, K7   (16sts)
- 114th row: K1, P14, K1
- 115th row: K3, inc in next, K7, inc in next, K1, K2tog, K1   (17sts)
- 116th row: K1, P15, K1
- 117th row: K9, inc in next, K7   (18sts)
- 118th row: K1, P16, K1
- 119th row: K
- 120th row: K1, P16, K1
- 121st row: K9, inc in next, K8   (19sts)
- 122nd row: K1, P17, K1
- 123rd row: K16, K2tog, K1   (18sts)
- 124th row: K1, P16, K1
- 125th row: K
- 126th row: K1, P16, K1
- 127th row: K

- 128th row: KI,PI6, KI
- 129th row: K
- 130th row: KI, PI4, P2tog, KI (I7sts)
- CHANGE TO COLOURS 8 & 9
- 131st row: K
- 132nd row: K
- CHANGE TO COLOUR 6
- 133rd row: K
- 134th row: KI, PI5, KI
- 135th row: KI4, K2tog, KI (I6sts)
- 136th row: KI, PI4, KI
- 137th row: K
- 138th row: KI, PI4, KI
- CHANGE TO COLOURS 8 & 9
- 139th row: K
- 140th row: K
- 141st row: K
- Cast off

To make up: Darn in ends. Fold sleeve in half, at shoulder tag mark. Match up the other two tags and gather up at this point. Sew sleeves into over-robe matching the shoulder tag to shoulder seam, and the gathered point of sleeve at armpit. Using COLOUR 10, work a row of 12, double-crochet around the cuff of sleeve. Work second row, with 2 chain loops into each double-crochet.

*Tip: Insert small piece of wadding into sleeve to create puffed shape.

FUR COLLAR OF OVER-ROBE

COLOUR 10
- Size 9/3.75mm needles

ROWS:	RIGHT SIDE:	LEFT SIDE:
	Cast on 3	Cast on 3
I	K	K
2	PI, KI, PI	PI, KI, PI
	Repeat row 2 (x4)	Repeat row 2 (x4)
7	Inc in Ist, KI, PI (4sts)	PI, KI, inc in last (4sts)
8	Work I & I MS starting with P	Work I & I MS starting with K
9	Work I & I MS starting with K	Work I & I MS starting with P
	Repeat rows 8 & 9 (x3)	Repeat rows 8 & 9 (x3)
16	As row 8	As row 8
17	Inc in Ist, PI, KI, PI (5sts)	PI, KI, PI, inc in last (5sts)
	Work 9 rows I & I MS starting with P	Work 9 rows I & I MS starting with P
27	Inc in Ist, KI, PI, KI, PI (6sts)	PI, KI, PI, KI, inc in last (6sts)
28	Work I & I MS starting with P	Work I & I MS starting with K
29	Work I & I MS starting with K	Work I & I MS starting with P
	Repeat rows 28 & 29 (x4)	Repeat rows 28 & 29 (x4)
38	Repeat row 28	Repeat row 28
39	Inc in Ist, PI, KI, PI,KI, PI (7sts)	PI, KI, PI,KI, PI, inc in last (7sts)
	Work II rows I & I MS starting with P	Work I & I MS starting with P
51	Inc in Ist (KI, PI) to end (8sts)	(PI, KI) to last, inc in last (8sts)
52	Work I & I MS starting with P	Work I & I MS starting with K
53	Work I & I MS starting with K	Work I & I MS starting with P
	Repeat row 52 & 53 (x4)	Repeat row 52 & 53 (x4)
62	Repeat row 52	Repeat row 52
63	Inc in Ist, (PI, KI) to end (9sts)	(PI, KI) to last, inc in last (9sts)
	Work 9 rows I & I MS starting with P	Work 9 rows I & I MS starting with P
73	Inc in Ist, (KI, PI) to end (10sts)	(PI, KI) to last, inc in last (10sts)
74	Work I & I MS starting with P	Work I & I MS starting with K
75	Work I & I MS starting with K	Work I & I MS starting with P
	Repeat row 74 & 75 (x2)	Repeat row 74 & 75 (x2)
80	Repeat row 74, cast on 9	Repeat row 74
	Set aside and work on left side:	

- Starting at the straight edge of the left side, work I & I MS starting with P on I0sts from left side, 9 cast on sts, I0sts from right side   (29sts)
- Work 18 rows I & I MS starting each row with P
- Cast off in MS

To make up: Brush with teasel-brush to make fluffy. Join to front edges and back neck of over-robe.
Dress doll.

CHAIN OF OFFICE

Use beads, gold lace, old jewellery to form a semi-circle. Stitch at shoulders.

HAIR

COLOUR 7

- Size 10/3.25mm needles

- Cast on 10
- 1st row: K
- 2nd row: P
- 3rd row: K row – inc in 1st & last (12sts)
- 4th row: P
- Repeat rows 3 & 4 (x5)   (22sts)
- Cast off

To make up: Fit to back of head. Stitch in place.

BEARD

COLOUR 7

- Size 10/3.25mm needles

- Cast on 30
- 1st row: K
- 2nd row: Cast off 7, P15, turn –
- 3rd row: K16, turn –
- 4th row: (K2tog)x8
- Cast off

To make up: Sew the cast-off edge around face to form the underside of the beard. Run a wool thread along the length of the opposite edge, pulling gently so that the beard gathers slightly to frame the lower part of the face. Pin and stitch in place.

HAT

COLOUR 11

- Size 10/3.25mm double-ended needles

BRIM

- Cast on 44
- Put on set of 4 needles, joining into circle
- 1st row: K
- 2nd row: K
- 3rd row: (K3, inc in next)x11   (55sts)
- 4th row: K
- Cast off

CROWN

- Cast on 43
- Put on set of 4 needles, joining into circle
- Work 4 rows K
- 5th row: K1, (K2tog, K2)x10, K2tog (32sts)
- Work 4 rows K
- 10th row: (K2tog)x16   (16sts)
- Work 2 rows K
- 13th row: (K2tog)x8   (8sts)
- 14th row: (K2tog)x4   (4sts)
- Pull wool through

To make up: Sew the crown to smaller edge of the brim. Embroider a zigzag pattern onto brim with COLOURS 8 & 9, used together, and decorate with beads. Trim edge of hat with small feathers, which overlap and run in the same direction. Attach one longer feather to trail over the right side.

TO CREATE FACE

Nose and ears are crochet chains, stitched to head. Eyes are blue yarn with black bead at centre. Add eyebrows in the same yarn as the beard, and add mouth in appropriate colour.

You will need

MATERIALS:★

Colour Codes:
1 Rowan Baby Merino Silk DK
(Shade SH674 – Shell Pink) – For Body
2 Debbie Bliss Baby Cashmerino
(Shade 340300 – Black) – For Boots
3 Debbie Bliss Rialto Lace
(Shade 44003 – Grey) – For Suit
4 Debbie Bliss Rialto Lace
(Shade 44005 – Black) – For Ties,
Belts & Pocket Tops
5 Patons Fairytale Dreamtime Pure
Wool 2-Ply (Shade 00051 – White) –
For Shirt
6 Debbie Bliss Cashmerino (Shade
340011 – Dark Brown) – For Hair

Black beads for jacket buttons & eyes
Small white beads for shirt fronts
Yarn for creating facial features
Stuffing

NEEDLES:

Size 10/3.25mm
Size 13/2.25mm
Size 14/2.00mm
Crochet hook – 4.00/4.50mm
Darning needle

*Please note: These materials are
used for ALL the individual Beatles'
patterns.*

The Beatles

John, Paul, George and Ringo are Liverpool's finest sons. When they formed their group in 1960, no one could have guessed how popular and successful The Beatles would become. The music they produced spoke to a new generation and turned them from four young Scouse lads into global superstars. Manager Brian Epstein nurtured them in the early years and producer George Martin helped them realise their musical potential at EMI's Abbey Road Studios in London. And when 'Please Please Me' went to No.1 there was no going back. 'She Loves You' soon became their first million-selling single and Beatlemania took over the world.

John Lennon and Paul McCartney jointly penned the majority of the work and are one of the most successful songwriting duos of all time. But, of course, The Beatles would not be The Beatles without the contributions of George Harrison and Ringo Starr. The combination of their unique talents produced a legacy that will live forever. And with a staggering 2 billion plus records sold worldwide, we like to remember them as they started out, the cheeky, fun-loving boys with a talent that would make them fab forever.

John Lennon

When John Winston Lennon was born in 1940, war was raging throughout Europe. His young life was also to prove pretty traumatic at times, and after his mother and his merchant seaman father separated, young John went to live with his Aunt Mimi, although his mother Julia visited him regularly. A creative boy, John also liked to be a bit of a prankster but he and school really didn't get along. Then, in 1957, John Lennon met Paul McCartney and the legendary songwriting duo was born.

After the incredible and unbelievably creative years with The Beatles when he would help create a body of work that will live on forever, John Lennon embarked on a solo career that would bring more success and critical acclaim. He had fully embraced the Sixties with all that it brought,

and as the decade ended, Lennon married Yoko Ono and a new era began for him.

John Lennon is remembered not only for his music but also for his campaigns. He made his views on the Vietnam War known and held anti-establishment views on many other subjects, much to the annoyance of the political elite who came to realise the power Lennon had to communicate. John Lennon survived FBI surveillance and attempts to have him deported from the US. Then, just as he was getting back to music after his virtual retirement from it, John Lennon was shot dead outside his New York home at forty years of age. It is a loss that was hard to comprehend at the time but his musical legacy and his message to the world live on.

BODY

COLOUR 1
Size 10/3.25mm needles

BODY – FRONT
- Cast on 16
- 1st row: K
- 2nd row: P
- 3rd row: K1, inc in next, K12, inc in next, K1   (18sts)
- Work 3 rows SS starting with P
- 7th row: K1, K2tog, K2, K2tog, K4, K2tog, K2, K2tog, K1   (14sts)
- Work 3 rows SS starting with P
- 11th row: K2, inc in next, K8, inc in next, K2   (16sts)
- 12th row: P
- 13th row: Inc in 1st, K3, inc in next, K6, inc in next, K3, inc in last   (20sts)
- Work 5 rows SS starting with P
- 19th row: K1, sl1, K1, psso, K14, K2tog, K1   (18sts)
- Work 3 rows SS starting with P
- 23rd row: K1, sl1, K1, psso, K12, K2tog, K1   (16sts)
- 24th row: P1, P2tog, P10, P2tog, P1   (14sts)
- 25th row: K1, sl1, K1, psso, K8, K2tog, K1   (12sts)
- 26th row: P
- Cast off

BODY – BACK
- Cast on 16
- 1st row: K
- 2nd row: P
- 3rd row: K2, inc in next, K1, inc in next, K6, inc in next, K1, inc in next, K2   (20sts)
- 4th row: P
- 5th row: K3, inc in next, K1, inc in next, K8, inc in next, K1, inc in next, K3   (24sts)
- Work 3 rows SS starting with P

- 9th row: K1, K2tog, K18, K2tog, K1   (22sts)
- 10th row: P
- 11th row: K2, K2tog, K1, K2tog, K8, K2tog, K1, K2tog, K2   (18sts)
- 12th row: P
- 13th row: (K2, K2tog)x4, K2   (14sts)
- Work 5 rows SS starting with P
- 19th row: K1, inc in next, K4, inc in next, inc in next, K4, inc in next, K1   (18sts)
- Work 7 rows SS starting with P
- 27th row: K1, sl1, K1, psso, K12, K2tog, K1   (16sts)
- 28th row: P1, P2tog, P10, P2tog, P1   (14sts)
- 29th row: K1, sl1, K1, psso, K8, K2tog, K1   (12sts)
- 30th row: P
- Cast off

To make up: Join front to back. Stuff.

ARMS – MAKE TWO

COLOUR 1
- Size 10/3.25mm needles

WORKING FROM SHOULDER
TO WRIST
- Cast on 5
- 1st row: K
- 2nd row: P
- 3rd row: K row – inc in 1st & last   (7sts)
- 4th row: P
- 5th row: K row – inc in 1st & last   (9sts)
- 6th row: P
- Work 26 rows

TO CREATE LEFT HAND
- 33rd row: K2, put 2 on pin, K5
- 34th row: P to end bringing 2 sections together   (7sts)

- 35th row: K
- 36th row: P
- 37th row: K2tog, K2tog, K2tog, K1
- 38th row: P2tog, P2tog
- Pull thread through

TO CREATE RIGHT HAND
- 33rd row: K5, put 2 on pin, K2   (7sts)
- 34th row: P
- 35th row: K
- 36th row: P
- 37th row: K1, K2tog, K2tog, K2tog
- 38th row: P2tog, P2tog
- Pull thread through

THUMB – SAME FOR BOTH HANDS
- Put 2sts from pin on double-ended needle
- Join thread, K2
- K2tog as i-cord
- Pull thread through

To make up: Join seams. Stuff. Add to body.

BOOTS AND LEGS – MAKE TWO

COLOUR 2
- Size 10/3.25mm needles
-
- Cast on 24
- 1st row: K
- 2nd row: P
- 3rd row: K10, K2tog, K2tog, K10   (22sts)
- 4th row: P10, P2tog, P10   (21sts)
- 5th row: K5, (K2tog, K1)x3, K2tog, K5   (17sts)
- 6th row: P
- 7th row: K4, cast off 9, K3   (8sts)
- 8th row: P, pulling 2 sections of 4sts together

- Work 4 rows SS starting with K
- 13th row: K1, inc in next, K4, inc in next, K1   (10sts)
- 14th row: P
- Break wool, JOIN COLOUR 1
- Work 6 rows SS starting with K
- 21st row: K1, inc in next, K6, inc in next, K1   (12sts)
- Work 26 rows SS starting with P
- Cast off

CREATING HEEL OF BOOT

Stitch back seam of boots
Pick-up 8 stitches along heel edge of boot from right to left – RS facing. Turn –

- 1st row: Cast on 1, P9
- 2nd row: Cast on 1, K10
- 3rd row: P1, (P2tog)x4, P1   (6sts)
- 4th row: K1, K2tog, K2tog, K1   (4sts)
- Cast off

To make up: Sew-up sole of boot and heel – stuff boot. Join leg seam & stuff. Wet boot with warm water, squeeze, shape and dry.

*Tip: Stuff boots with offcuts of black wool rather than white wadding, which tends to show through.

HEAD

COLOUR 1

- Size 10/3.25mm needles

HEAD – FRONT

- Cast on 6sts
- 1st row: P
- 2nd row: K
- 3rd row: P row – inc in 1st & last   (8sts)
- 4th row: K
- 5th row: P row – inc in 1st & last   (10sts)

- 6th row: K
- 7th row: P row – inc in 1st & last   (12sts)
- 8th row: K
- 9th row: P row – inc in 1st & last   (14sts)
- Work 8 rows SS starting with K
- 18th row: K1, sl1, K1, psso, K8, K2tog, K1   (12sts)
- 19th row: P
- 20th row: K1, sl1, K1, psso, K6, K2tog, K1   (10sts)
- 21st row: P
- Cast off

HEAD – BACK

- Cast on 6
- 1st row: K
- 2nd row: P
- 3rd row: K row – inc in 1st & last   (8sts)
- 4th row: P
- 5th row: Inc in 1st, K2, K2tog, K2, inc in last   (9sts)
- 6th row: P
- CHANGE TO COLOUR 6
- 7th row: Inc in 1st, K3, inc in next, K3, inc in last   (12sts)
- 8th row: P
- 9th row: Inc in 1st, K4, inc in next, inc in next, K4, inc in last   (16sts)
- Work 7 rows SS starting with P
- 17th row: Inc in 1st, K3, inc in next, K1, inc in next, K2, inc in next, K1, inc in next, K3, inc in last   (22sts)
- Work 3 rows SS starting with P
- 21st row: (K2tog, K1)x3, K2tog, K2tog, (K1, K2tog)x3   (14sts)
- 22nd row: (P2tog, P2)x3, P2tog   (10sts)
- Cast off

To make up: Join front and back. Stuff. Attach all parts to body.

SHIRT FRONT

WORKING FROM HIP TO SHOULDER
COLOUR 5

- Size 13/2.25mm needles

- Cast on 24
- Work 22 rows SS starting with K
- 23rd row: K – inc in 1st and last   (26sts)
- Work 12 rows SS starting with P
- Cast off

To make up: Stitch onto body front at shoulders and hips. Add 3 to 4 small white beads for buttons.

COLLAR

COLOUR 5

- Size 13/2.25mm needles
-
- Cast on 26
- Work 8 rows SS starting with K
- Cast off

To make up: Fold and iron under a damp cloth. Attach around neck and to shirt front.

TROUSERS

COLOUR 3

- Size 13/2.25mm needles

- Cast on 25
- Work 44 rows SS starting with K
- 45th row: K1, inc in next, K21, inc in next, K1   (27sts)
- Work 9 rows SS starting with P
- 55th row: K1, inc in next, K23, inc in next, K1   (29sts)
- 56th row: P
- 57th row: K1, inc in next, K1, inc in next, K21, inc in next, K1, inc in next, K1   (33sts)

- 58th row: P
- 59th row: Cast off 2, K30   (31sts)
- 60th row: Cast off 2, K28   (29sts)
- Work 10 rows SS starting with K
- 71st row: K2tog, K25 K2tog   (27sts)
- 72nd row: P
- CHANGE TO COLOUR 4 FOR BELT DETAIL
- 73rd row: K
- 74th row: P
- CHANGE TO COLOUR 3
- 75th row: K
- 76th row: P
- Cast off

Repeat rows 1 to 76 for second leg.

To make up: Join inside leg seams. Join crotch. Dress doll.

JACKET
COLOUR 3
- Size 13/2.25mm needles

- Cast on 53
- 1st row: P
- 2nd row: Inc in 1st, K51, inc in last (55sts)
- 3rd row: Inc in 1st, P53, inc in last (57sts)
- 4th row: Inc in 1st, K55, inc in last (59sts)
- Work 7 rows SS starting with P

FOR TOP EDGES OF POCKET FLAPS:
- 12th row: K6 in COLOUR 3, K9 in COLOUR 4, K29 in COLOUR 3, K9 in COLOUR 4, K6 in COLOUR 3
- 13th row: P6 in COLOUR 3, P9 in COLOUR 4, P29 in COLOUR 3, P9 in COLOUR 4, P6 in COLOUR 3
- CONTINUE IN COLOUR 3
- 14th row: K
- 15th row: P

- 16th row: K15, K2tog, K25, K2tog, K15 (57sts)
- Work 21 rows SS starting with P

WORKING ON FRONT RIGHT – SPLITTING OFF FOR ARMHOLES
- 38th row: K14, K2tog   (15sts)
- Put remaining st on pin
- 39th row: P2tog, P13   (14sts)
- Work 6 rows SS starting with K
- 46th row: Cast off 6, K7   (8sts)
- 47th row: P
- 48th row: K2tog, K6
- 49th row: Cast off 3, P3   (4sts)
- 50th row: K2tog, K2   (3sts)
- Cast off

WORKING ON LEFT FRONT – WS FACING
- Put 16 of held stitches on needle – hold rest on pin
- 38th row: P14, P2tog   (15sts)
- 39th row: K2tog, K13   (14sts)
- Work 6 rows SS starting with P
- 46th row: Cast off 6, P7   (8sts)
- 47th row: K
- 48th row: P2tog, P6   (7sts)
- 49th row: Cast off 3, K3   (4sts)
- 50th row: P2tog, P2   (3sts)
- Cast off

WORKING ON JACKET BACK ON REMAINING 25STS
- RS FACING
- 38th row: K2tog, K21, K2tog   (23sts)
- Work 3 rows SS starting with P
- 42nd row: K row – inc in 1st and last (25sts)
- Work 7 rows SS starting with P
- Cast off

To make up: Join shoulder seams.

JACKET SLEEVES
COLOUR 5
- Size 13/2.25mm needles

- Cast on 20
- 1st row: K
- 2nd row: P
- CHANGE TO COLOUR 3
- Work 36 rows SS starting with K
- 39th row: Cast off 4, K15   (16sts)
- 40th row: Cast off 4, P11   (12sts)
- 41st row: K2tog, K8, K2tog   (10sts)
- Work 3 rows SS starting with P
- 45th row: K2tog, K2tog, K2, K2tog, K2tog   (6sts)
- 46th row: P2tog, P2, P2tog   (4sts)
- Cast off

To make up: Join seams. Inset in jacket. Dress Doll. Add beads for buttons on jacket front.

TIE
COLOUR 4
- Size 14/2.00mm

- Cast on 3
- Work 24 rows SS starting with K
- 25th row: K1, inc in next, K1   (4sts)
- Work 43 rows SS starting with P
- 69th row: K2tog, K2tog
- 70th row: K2tog – pull wool through

To make up: Steam press flat. Fold in half making a knot and stitch in place around neck.

HAIR
Use photographs to reference the slight differences in the hairstyles. Cut lengths of COLOUR 6. Separate strands and press flat with a steam iron. Thread a darning needle with 3 or 4 strands

at a time and overlay long stitches from crown to nape of neck, using the coloured back of head as a guideline, and in loops or loose lengths for fringes.

*Tip: Make over-long and trim when fringe looks thick enough.

TO CREATE FACE

Add beads for eyes. The nose and ears are fashioned from crocheted chains of the flesh-coloured wool. Pin and stitch on when you feel you have a good likeness. Add eyebrows and mouth.

Paul McCartney

The McCartney bit of Lennon and McCartney is, of course, Sir James Paul McCartney, who was born in Liverpool in 1942. His astonishing career, all the way from The Beatles to Wings to his solo work, has made him a living legend and one of the world's most revered musicians. His success post–Beatles has been incredible, including 'Band on the Run', 'With a Little Luck' and 'Mull of Kintyre'. And, yes, 'Ebony and Ivory' with Stevie Wonder, which a lot of people liked for reasons which a lot of other people never really got. But what is certain is that the silly love songs, and the others, sold by the million.

Unlike John Lennon, the young Paul McCartney did well at school and gained admission to grammar school in Liverpool, where he met George Harrison. Like Lennon, Paul McCartney lost his mother when he was still young but his father, a jazz musician, always encouraged young Paul to play music. Paul was fifteen when he met John and the two young men clicked.

Over the decades, Paul McCartney's love life has often been in the headlines. He dated Jane Asher in the Sixties then married Linda Eastman, a photographer who worked with many of the bands at that time. Paul and the famously vegetarian Linda had a happy marriage and three children together until Linda's untimely death in 1998 at the age of fifty-six. McCartney's subsequent marriage to Heather Mills made headlines for all the wrong reasons and their divorce six years later was bitter and very public. His marriage in 2011 to Nancy Shevell has been an altogether happier time in his life and he continues to live a fab life as one of the most famous musicians on the planet.

BODY

COLOUR 1
Size 10/3.25mm needles

BODY – FRONT
- Cast on 16
- 1st row: K
- 2nd row: P
- 3rd row: K1, inc in next, K12, inc in next, K1   (18sts)
- Work 3 rows SS starting with P
- 7th row: K1, K2tog, K2, K2tog, K4, K2tog, K2, K2tog, K1   (14sts)
- Work 3 rows SS starting with P
- 11th row: K2, inc in next, K8, inc in next, K2   (16sts)
- 12th row: P
- 13th row: Inc in 1st, K3, inc in next, K6, inc in next, K3, inc in last   (20sts)
- Work 5 rows SS starting with P
- 19th row: K1, sl1, K1, psso, K14, K2tog, K1   (18sts)
- Work 3 rows SS starting with P
- 23rd row: K1, sl1, K1, psso, K12, K2tog, K1   (16sts)
- 24th row: P1, P2tog, P10, P2tog, P1   (14sts)
- 25th row: K1, sl1, K1, psso, K8, K2tog, K1   (12sts)
- 26th row: P
- Cast off

BODY – BACK
- Cast on 16
- 1st row: K
- 2nd row: P
- 3rd row: K2, inc in next, K1, inc in next, K6, inc in next, K1, inc in next, K2   (20sts)
- 4th row: P
- 5th row: K3, inc in next, K1, inc in next, K8, inc in next, K1, inc in next, K3   (24sts)
- Work 3 rows SS starting with P

- 9th row: K1, K2tog, K18, K2tog, K1   (22sts)
- 10th row P
- 11th row: K2, K2tog, K1, K2tog, K8, K2tog, K1, K2tog, K2   (18sts)
- 12th row: P
- 13th row: (K2, K2tog)x4, K2   (14sts)
- Work 5 rows SS starting with P
- 19th row: K1, inc in next, K4, inc in next, inc in next, K4, inc in next, K1   (18sts)
- Work 7 rows SS starting with P
- 27th row: K1, sl1, K1, psso, K12, K2tog, K1   (16sts)
- 28th row: P1, P2tog, P10, P2tog, P1   (14sts)
- 29th row: K1, sl1, K1, psso, K8, K2tog, K1   (12sts)
- 30th row: P
- Cast off

To make up: Join front to back. Stuff.

ARMS – MAKE TWO

COLOUR 1
- Size 10/3.25mm needles

WORKING FROM SHOULDER TO WRIST
- Cast on 5
- 1st row: K
- 2nd row: P
- 3rd row: K row – inc in 1st & last   (7sts)
- 4th row: P
- 5th row: K row – inc in 1st & last   (9sts)
- 6th row: P
- Work 26 rows

TO CREATE LEFT HAND
- 33rd row: K2, put 2 on pin, K5
- 34th row: P to end bringing 2 sections together   (7sts)

- 35th row: K
- 36th row: P
- 37th row: K2tog, K2tog, K2tog, K1
- 38th row: P2tog, P2tog
- Pull thread through

TO CREATE RIGHT HAND
- 33rd row: K5, put 2 on pin, K2   (7sts)
- 34th row: P
- 35th row: K
- 36th row: P
- 37th row: K1, K2tog, K2tog, K2tog
- 38th row: P2tog, P2tog
- Pull thread through

THUMB – SAME FOR BOTH HANDS
- Put 2sts from pin on double-ended needle
- Join thread, K2
- K2tog as i-cord
- Pull thread through

To make up: Join seams. Stuff. Add to body.

BOOTS AND LEGS – MAKE TWO

COLOUR 2
- Size 10/3.25mm needles

- Cast on 24
- 1st row: K
- 2nd row: P
- 3rd row: K10, K2tog, K2tog, K10   (22sts)
- 4th row: P10, P2tog, P10   (21sts)
- 5th row: K5, (K2tog, K1)x3, K2tog, K5   (17sts)
- 6th row: P
- 7th row: K4, cast off 9, K3   (8sts)
- 8th row: P, pulling 2 sections of 4sts together
- Work 4 rows SS starting with K

- 13th row: K1, inc in next, K4, inc in next, K1   (10sts)
- 14th row: P
- Break wool, JOIN COLOUR 1
- Work 6 rows SS starting with K
- 21st row: K1, inc in next, K6, inc in next, K1   (12sts)
- Work 26 rows SS starting with P
- Cast off

CREATING HEEL OF BOOT
- Stitch back seam of boots
- Pick-up 8 stitches along heel edge of boot from right to left – RS facing Turn -
- 1st row: Cast on 1, P9
- 2nd row: Cast on 1, K10
- 3rd row: P1, (P2tog)x4, P1   (6sts)
- 4th row: K1, K2tog, K2tog, K1   (4sts)
- Cast off

To make up: Sew-up sole of boot and heel – stuff boot. Join leg seam & stuff. Wet boot with warm water, squeeze, shape and dry.

*Tip: Stuff boots with offcuts of black wool rather than white wadding, which tends to show through.

HEAD

COLOUR 1
- Size 10/3.25mm needles

HEAD – FRONT
- Cast on 6
- 1st row: K
- 2nd row: P
- 3rd row: K row – inc in 1st & last (8sts)
- 4th row: P
- 5th row: K row – inc in 1st & last (10sts)
- 6th row: P

- 7th row: K row – inc in 1st & last (12sts)
- 8th row: P
- 9th row: K row – inc in 1st & last (14sts)
- Work 7 rows SS starting with P
- 17th row: K1, sl1, K1, psso, K8, K2tog, K1   (12sts)
- 18th row: P
- 19th row: K1, sl1, K1, psso, K6, K2tog, K1   (10sts)
- 20th row: P
- Cast off

HEAD – BACK
- Cast on 6
- 1st row: K
- 2nd row: P
- 3rd row: K row – inc in 1st & last (8sts)
- 4th row: P
- 5th row: Inc in 1st, K2, K2tog, K2, inc in last   (9sts)
- 6th row: P
- CHANGE TO COLOUR 6
- 7th row: Inc in 1st, K3, inc in next, K3, inc in last   (12sts)
- 8th row: P
- 9th row: Inc in 1st, K4, inc in next, inc in next, K4, inc in last   (16sts)
- Work 5 rows SS starting with P
- 15th row: Inc in 1st, K3, inc in next, K1, inc in next, K2, inc in next, K1, inc in next, K3, inc in last   (22sts)
- Work 3 rows SS starting with P
- 19th row: (K2tog, K1)x3, K2tog, K2tog, (K1, K2tog)x3   (14sts)
- 20th row: (P2tog, P2)x3, P2tog (10sts)
- Cast off

To make up: Join front and back. Stuff. Attach all parts to body.

SHIRT FRONT
WORKING FROM HIP TO SHOULDER
COLOUR 5
- Size 13/2.25mm needles

- Cast on 24
- Work 22 rows SS starting with K
- 23rd row: K row – inc in 1st and last (26sts)
- Work 12 rows SS starting with P
- Cast off

To make up: Stitch onto body front at shoulders and hips. Add 3 to 4 small white beads for buttons.

COLLAR
COLOUR 5
- Size 13/2.25mm needles
-
- Cast on 26
- Work 8 rows SS starting with K
- Cast off

To make up: Fold and iron under a damp cloth. Attach around neck and to shirt front.

TROUSERS
COLOUR 3
- Size 13/2.25mm needles
-
- Cast on 25
- Work 44 rows SS starting with K
- 45th row: K1, inc in next, K21, inc in next, K1   (27sts)
- Work 9 rows SS starting with P
- 55th row: K1, inc in next, K23, inc in next, K1   (29sts)
- 56th row: P
- 57th row: K1, inc in next, K1, inc in next, K21, inc in next, K1, inc in next, K1   (33sts)

- 58th row: P
- 59th row: Cast off 2, K30   (31sts)
- 60th row: Cast off 2, K28   (29sts)
- Work 10 rows SS starting with K
- 71st row: K2tog, K25 K2tog   (27sts)
- 72nd row: P
- CHANGE TO COLOUR 4 FOR BELT DETAIL
- 73rd row: K
- 74th row: P
- CHANGE TO COLOUR 3
- 75th row: K
- 76th row: P
- Cast off

Repeat rows 1 to 76 for second leg.

To make up: Join inside leg seams. Join crotch. Dress doll.

JACKET

COLOUR 3
- Size 13/2.25mm needles

- Cast on 53
- 1st row: P
- 2nd row: Inc in 1st, K51, inc in last (55sts)
- 3rd row: Inc in 1st, P53, inc in last (57sts)
- 4th row: Inc in 1st, K55, inc in last (59sts)
- Work 7 rows SS starting with P

FOR TOP EDGES OF POCKET FLAPS:
- 12th row: K6 in COLOUR 3, K9 in COLOUR 4, K29 in COLOUR 3, K9 in COLOUR 4, K6 in COLOUR 3
- 13th row: P6 in COLOUR 3, P9 in COLOUR 4, P29 in COLOUR 3, P9 in COLOUR 4, P6 in COLOUR 3
- CONTINUE IN COLOUR 3
- 14th row: K
- 15th row: P

- 16th row: K15, K2tog, K25, K2tog, K15 (57sts)
- Work 21 rows SS starting with P

WORKING ON FRONT RIGHT – SPLITTING OFF FOR ARMHOLES
- 38th row: K14, K2tog   (15sts)
- Put remaining st on pin
- 39th row: P2tog, P13   (14sts)
- Work 6 rows SS starting with K
- 46th row: Cast off 6, K7   (8sts)
- 47th row: P
- 48th row: K2tog, K6
- 49th row: Cast off 3, P3   (4sts)
- 50th row: K2tog, K2   (3sts)
- Cast off

WORKING ON LEFT FRONT – WS FACING
- Put 16 of held stitches on needle – hold rest on pin
- 38th row: P14, P2tog   (15sts)
- 39th row: K2tog, K13   (14sts)
- Work 6 rows SS starting with P
- 46th row: Cast off 6, P7   (8sts)
- 47th row: K
- 48th row: P2tog, P6   (7sts)
- 49th row: Cast off 3, K3   (4sts)
- 50th row: P2tog, P2   (3sts)
- Cast off

WORKING ON JACKET BACK ON REMAINING 25STS RS FACING
- 38th row: K2tog, K21, K2tog   (23sts)
- Work 3 rows SS starting with P
- 42nd row: K row – inc in 1st and last (25sts)
- Work 7 rows SS starting with P
- Cast off

To make up: Join shoulder seams.

JACKET SLEEVES

COLOUR 5
- Size 13/2.25mm needles

- Cast on 20
- 1st row: K
- 2nd row: P
- CHANGE TO COLOUR 3
- Work 36 rows SS starting with K
- 39th row: Cast off 4, K15   (16sts)
- 40th row: Cast off 4, P11   (12sts)
- 41st row: K2tog, K8, K2tog   (10sts)
- Work 3 rows SS starting with P
- 45th row: K2tog, K2tog, K2, K2tog, K2tog   (6sts)
- 46th row: P2tog, P2, P2tog   (4sts)
- Cast off

To make up: Join seams. Inset in jackets. Dress Doll. Add beads for buttons on jacket front.

TIE

COLOUR 4
- Size 14/2.00mm needles

- Cast on 3
- Work 24 rows SS starting with K
- 25th row: K1, inc in next, K1   (4sts)
- Work 43 rows SS starting with P
- 69th row: K2tog, K2tog   (2sts)
- 70th row: K2tog – pull wool through

To make up: Steam press flat. Fold in half making a knot and stitch in place around neck.

HAIR

Use photographs to reference the slight differences in the hairstyles. Cut lengths of COLOUR 6. Separate strands and press flat with a steam iron. Thread a darning needle with 3 or 4 strands

at a time and overlay long stitches from crown to nape of neck, using the coloured back of head as a guideline, and in loops or loose lengths for fringes.

*Tip: Make over-long and trim when fringe looks thick enough.

TO CREATE FACE

Add beads for eyes. The nose and ears are fashioned from crocheted chains of the flesh-coloured wool. Pin and stitch on when you feel you have a good likeness. Add eyebrows and mouth.

George Harrison

George Harrison was the youngest member of The Beatles. He was also the youngest of four children born into a typical family in Liverpool. There was never much money around but, from an early age, his mother recognised his love of music and encouraged it. His father was a little more reluctant about his son's wish to pursue a career in music but he did buy him his first acoustic guitar and it all seemed to work out pretty well in the end.

After The Beatles, George Harrison was free to express himself in his own music, without the constrictions of Lennon and McCartney's near-monopoly on songwriting. The result was a remarkable outpouring of work which had both critical acclaim and commercial success. Harrison also continued to experiment with Eastern influences throughout his life, organised a Concert for Bangladesh in 1971 and carried on his solo career through the Seventies. Later, in 1988, Harrison co-founded the Traveling Wilburys with Roy Orbison, Jeff Lynne, Bob Dylan and Tom Petty and again enjoyed considerable success.

George Harrison survived a horrific attack by an assailant at his palatial Friar Park home in 1999, during which he received more than forty stab wounds, the attack only failing when his wife Olivia used a blunt instrument to incapacitate the intruder. Two years later, it was revealed that Harrison had cancer and he died in November 2001. His ashes were scattered on the River Ganges, ending a spiritual journey that had started in the heady days of the Swinging Sixties and ended all too young at the age of fifty-eight.

BODY

COLOUR 1

Size 10/3.25mm needles

BODY – FRONT

- Cast on 16
- 1st row: K
- 2nd row: P
- 3rd row: K1, inc in next, K12, inc in next, K1 (18sts)
- Work 3 rows SS starting with P
- 7th row: K1, K2tog, K2, K2tog, K4, K2tog, K2, K2tog, K1 (14sts)
- Work 3 rows SS starting with P
- 11th row: K2, inc in next, K8, inc in next, K2 (16sts)
- 12th row: P
- 13th row: Inc in 1st, K3, inc in next, K6, inc in next, K3, inc in last (20sts)
- Work 5 rows SS starting with P
- 19th row: K1, sl1, K1, psso, K14, K2tog, K1 (18sts)
- Work 3 rows SS starting with P
- 23rd row: K1, sl1, K1, psso, K12, K2tog, K1 (16sts)
- 24th row: P1, P2tog, P10, P2tog, P1 (14sts)
- 25th row: K1, sl1, K1, psso, K8, K2tog, K1 (12sts)
- 26th row: P
- Cast off

BODY – BACK

- Cast on 16
- 1st row: K
- 2nd row: P
- 3rd row: K2, inc in next, K1, inc in next, K6, inc in next, K1, inc in next, K2 (20sts)
- 4th row: P
- 5th row: K3, inc in next, K1, inc in next, K8, inc in next, K1, inc in next, K3 (24sts)
- Work 3 rows SS starting with P

- 9th row: K1, K2tog, K18, K2tog, K1 (22sts)
- 10th row: P
- 11th row: K2, K2tog, K1, K2tog, K8, K2tog, K1, K2tog, K2 (18sts)
- 12th row: P
- 13th row: (K2, K2tog)x4, K2 (14sts)
- Work 5 rows SS starting with P
- 19th row: K1, inc in next, K4, inc in next, inc in next, K4, inc in next, K1 (18sts)
- Work 7 rows SS starting with P
- 27th row: K1, sl1, K1, psso, K12, K2tog, K1 (16sts)
- 28th row: P1, P2tog, P10, P2tog, P1 (14sts)
- 29th row: K1, sl1, K1, psso, K8, K2tog, K1 (12sts)
- 30th row: P
- Cast off

To make up: Join front to back. Stuff.

ARMS – MAKE TWO

COLOUR 1

- Size 10/3.25mm needles

- WORKING FROM SHOULDER TO WRIST
- Cast on 5
- 1st row: K
- 2nd row: P
- 3rd row: K row – inc in 1st & last (7sts)
- 4th row: P
- 5th row: K row – inc in 1st & last (9sts)
- 6th row: P
- Work 26 rows

TO CREATE LEFT HAND

- 33rd row: K2, put 2 on pin, K5
- 34th row: P to end bringing 2 sections together (7sts)

- 35th row: K
- 36th row: P
- 37th row: K2tog, K2tog, K2tog, K1
- 38th row: P2tog, P2tog
- Pull thread through

TO CREATE RIGHT HAND

- 33rd row: K5, put 2 on pin, K2 (7sts)
- 34th row: P
- 35th row: K
- 36th row: P
- 37th row: K1, K2tog, K2tog, K2tog
- 38th row: P2tog, P2tog
- Pull thread through

THUMB – SAME FOR BOTH HANDS

- Put 2sts from pin on double-ended needle
- Join thread, K2
- K2tog as i-cord
- Pull thread through

To make up: Join seams. Stuff. Add to body.

BOOTS AND LEGS – MAKE TWO

COLOUR 2

- Size 10/3.25mm needles

- Cast on 24
- 1st row: K
- 2nd row: P
- 3rd row: K10, K2tog, K2tog, K10 (22sts)
- 4th row: P10, P2tog, P10 (21sts)
- 5th row: K5, (K2tog, K1)x3, K2tog, K5 (17sts)
- 6th row: P
- 7th row: K4, cast off 9, K3 (8sts)
- 8th row: P, pulling 2 sections of 4sts together

- Work 4 rows SS starting with K
- 13th row: K1, inc in next, K4, inc in next, K1   (10sts)
- 14th row: P
- Break wool, JOIN COLOUR 1
- Work 6 rows SS starting with K
- 21st row: K1, inc in next, K6, inc in next, K1   (12sts)
- Work 26 rows SS starting with P
- Cast off

CREATING HEEL OF BOOT
- Stitch back seam of boots
- Pick-up 8 stitches along heel edge of boot from right to left – RS facing. Turn --
- 1st row: Cast on 1,P9
- 2nd row: Cast on 1, K10
- 3rd row: (P1, P2tog)×4, P1   (6sts)
- 4th row: K1,K2tog, K2tog, K1   (4sts)
- Cast off

To make up: Sew-up sole of boot and heel – stuff boot. Join leg seam & stuff. Wet boot with warm water, squeeze, shape and dry.

*Tip: Stuff boots with offcuts of black wool rather than white wadding, which tends to show through.

HEAD

COLOUR 1
- Size 10/3.25mm needles

HEAD – FRONT
- Cast on 6
- 1st row: K
- 2nd row: P
- 3rd row: K row – inc in 1st & last (8sts)
- 4th row: P
- 5th row: K row – inc in 1st & last (10sts)

- 6th row: P
- 7th row: K row – inc in 1st & last (12sts)
- 8th row: P
- 9th row: K row – inc in 1st & last (14sts)
- Work 7 rows SS starting with P
- 17th row: K1, sl1, K1, psso K8, K2tog, K1   (12sts)
- 18th row: P
- 19th row: K1, sl1, K1, psso, K6, K2tog, K1   (10sts)
- 20th row: P
- Cast off

HEAD – BACK
- Cast on 6
- 1st row: K
- 2nd row: P
- 3rd row: K row – inc in 1st and last (8sts)
- 4th row: P
- 5th row: Inc in 1st, K2, K2tog, K2, inc in last   (9sts)
- 6th row: P
- CHANGE TO COLOUR 6
- 7th row: Inc in 1st, K3, inc in next, K3, inc in last   (12sts)
- 8th row: P
- 9th row: Inc in 1st, K4, inc in next, inc in next, K4, inc in last   (16sts)
- Work 5 rows SS starting with P
- 15th row: K5, K2tog, K2, K2tog, K5 (14sts)
- 16th row: P
- 17th row: K1, sl1, K1, psso, K8, K2tog, K1   (12sts)
- 18th row: P
- 19th row: K1, sl1, K1, psso, K6, K2tog, K1   (10sts)
- 20th row: P
- Cast off

To make up: Join front and back. Stuff. Attach all parts to body.

SHIRT FRONT

WORKING FROM HIP TO SHOULDER COLOUR 5
- Size 13/2.25mm needles

- Cast on 24
- Work 22 rows SS starting with K
- 23rd row: K row – inc in 1st and last (26sts)
- Work 12 rows SS starting with P
- Cast off
-
- To make up: Stitch onto body front at shoulders and hips. Add 3 to 4 small white beads for buttons.

COLLAR

COLOUR 5
- Size 13/2.25mm needles

- Cast on 26
- Work 8 rows SS starting with K
- Cast off

To make up: Fold and iron under a damp cloth. Attach around neck and to shirt front.

TROUSERS

COLOUR 3
- Size 13/2.25mm needles

- Cast on 25
- Work 44 rows SS starting with K
- 45th row: K1, inc in next, K21, inc in next, K1   (27sts)
- Work 9 rows SS starting with P
- 55th row: K1, inc in next, K23, inc in next, K1   (29sts)
- 56th row: P
- 57th row: K1, inc in next, K1, inc in next, K21, inc in next, K1, inc in next, K1   (33sts)

- 58th row: P
- 59th row: Cast off 2, K30   (31sts)
- 60th row: Cast off 2, K28   (29sts)
- Work 10 rows SS starting with K
- 71st row: K2tog, K25 K2tog   (27sts)
- 72nd row: P
- CHANGE TO COLOUR 4 FOR BELT DETAIL
- 73rd row: K
- 74th row: P
- CHANGE TO COLOUR 3
- 75th row: K
- 76th row: P
- Cast off

Repeat rows 1 to 76 for second leg.

To make up: Join inside leg seams. Join crotch. Dress doll.

JACKET

COLOUR 3
- Size 13/2.25mm needles

- Cast on 53
- 1st row: P
- 2nd row: Inc in 1st, K51, inc in last (55sts)
- 3rd row: Inc in 1st, P53, inc in last (57sts)
- 4th row: Inc in 1st, K55, inc in last (59sts)
- Work 7 rows SS starting with P

FOR TOP EDGES OF POCKET FLAPS:
- 12th row: K6 in COLOUR 3, K9 in COLOUR 4, K29 in COLOUR 3, K9 in COLOUR 4, K6 in COLOUR 3
- 13th row: P6 in COLOUR 3, P9 in COLOUR 4, P29 in COLOUR 3, P9 in COLOUR 4, P6 in COLOUR 3
- CONTINUE IN COLOUR 3
- 14th row: K
- 15th row: P

- 16th row: K15, K2tog, K25, K2tog, K15 (57sts)
- Work 21 rows SS starting with P

WORKING ON FRONT RIGHT – SPLITTING OFF FOR ARMHOLES
- 38th row: K14, K2tog   (15sts)
- Put remaining st on pin
- 39th row: P2tog, P13   (14sts)
- Work 6 rows SS starting with K
- 46th row: Cast off 6, K7   (8sts)
- 47th row: P
- 48th row: K2tog, K6
- 49th row: Cast off 3, P3   (4sts)
- 50th row: K2tog, K2   (3sts)
- Cast off

WORKING ON LEFT FRONT – WS FACING
- Put 16 of held stitches on needle – hold rest on pin
- 38th row: P14, P2tog   (15sts)
- 39th row: K2tog, K13
- Work 6 rows SS starting with P
- 46th row: Cast off 6, P7   (8sts)
- 47th row: K
- 48th row: P2tog, P6   (7sts)
- 49th row: Cast off 3, K3   (4sts)
- 50th row: P2tog, P2   (3sts)
- Cast off

WORKING ON JACKET BACK ON REMAINING 25STS RS FACING
- 38th row: K2tog, K21, K2tog   (23sts)
- Work 3 rows SS starting with P
- 42nd row: K row – inc in 1st and last (25sts)
- Work 7 rows SS starting with P
- Cast off

To make up: Join shoulder seams.

JACKET SLEEVES

COLOUR 5
- Size 13/2.25mm needles

- Cast on 20
- 1st row: K
- 2nd row: P
- CHANGE TO COLOUR 3
- Work 36 rows SS starting with K
- 39th row: Cast off 4, K15   (16sts)
- 40th row: Cast off 4, P11   (12sts)
- 41st row: K2tog, K8, K2tog   (10sts)
- Work 3 rows SS starting with P
- 45th row: K2tog, K2tog, K2, K2tog, K2tog   (6sts)
- 46th row: P2tog, P2, P2tog   (4sts)
- Cast off

To make up: Join seams. Inset in jacket. Dress Doll. Add beads for buttons on jacket front.

TIE

COLOUR 4
- Size 14/2.00mm needles

- Cast on 3
- Work 24 rows SS starting with K
- 25th row: K1, inc in next, K1   (4sts)
- Work 43 rows SS starting with P
- 69th row: K2tog, K2tog   (2sts)
- 70th row: K2tog – pull wool through

To make up: Steam press flat. Fold in half making a knot and stitch in place around neck.

HAIR

Use photographs to reference the slight differences in the hairstyles. Cut lengths of COLOUR 6. Separate strands and press flat with a steam iron. Thread a darning needle with 3 or 4 strands

at a time and overlay long stitches from crown to nape of neck, using the coloured back of head as a guideline, and in loops or loose lengths for fringes.

*Tip: Make over-long and trim when fringe looks thick enough.

TO CREATE FACE

Add beads for eyes. The nose and ears are fashioned from crocheted chains of the flesh-coloured wool. Pin and stitch on when you feel you have a good likeness. Add eyebrows and mouth.

Ringo Starr

Richard Starkey played drums and also sang lead vocals on several Beatles songs including the massive hit 'Yellow Submarine'. Born in 1940, his childhood was blighted by illness, including tuberculosis from which it took him several years to recover. His parents separated when he was young and he rarely saw his father thereafter. His mother Elsie, however, was a fierce supporter of her son and took on any job she had to in order to make ends meet. His childhood illnesses severely affected his schoolwork and, with all the time away from school, he never really caught up with his peers.

A late addition to The Beatles, Ringo was already in a successful band when he was approached to replace Pete Best. Best's sacking and Ringo's appointment did not go down too well with many fans but the Fab Four's line-up was completed with Ringo on drums.

After The Beatles, Ringo released various solo works, initially to commercial success but his later work did not find such big audiences. He did, however, find unexpected success as the voice of Thomas the Tank Engine, which introduced the legendary Beatle to a whole new audience. Ringo had three children with his first wife, Maureen Cox, and later married actress Barbara Bach, who played Anya Amasova in the 1977 Bond movie *The Spy Who Loved Me*. By any standards it has been quite a journey from the town where he was born to a life of ease where he has all he needs.

BODY

COLOUR 1
Size 10/3.25mm needles

BODY – FRONT
- Cast on 16
- 1st row: K
- 2nd row: P
- 3rd row: K1, inc in next, K12, inc in next, K1   (18sts)
- Work 3 rows SS starting with P
- 7th row: K1, K2tog, K2, K2tog, K4, K2tog, K2, K2tog, K1   (14sts)
- Work 3 rows SS starting with P
- 11th row: K2, inc in next, K8, inc in next, K2   (16sts)
- 12th row: P
- 13th row: Inc in 1st, K3, inc in next, K6, inc in next, K3, inc in last   (20sts)
- Work 5 rows SS starting with P
- 19th row: K1, sl1, K1, psso, K14, K2tog, K1   (18sts)
- Work 3 rows SS starting with P
- 23rd row: K1, sl1, K1, psso, K12, K2tog, K1   (16sts)
- 24th row: P1, P2tog, P10, P2tog, P1   (14sts)
- 25th row: K1, sl1, K1, psso, K8, K2tog, K1   (12sts)
- 26th row: P
- Cast off

BODY – BACK
- Cast on 16
- 1st row: K
- 2nd row: P
- 3rd row: K2, inc in next, K1, inc in next, K6, inc in next, K1, inc in next, K2   (20sts)
- 4th row: P
- 5th row: K3, inc in next, K1, inc in next, K8, inc in next, K1, inc in next, K3   (24sts)
- Work 3 rows SS starting with P

- 9th row: K1, K2tog, K18, K2tog, K1   (22sts)
- 10th row: P
- 11th row: K2, K2tog, K1, K2tog, K8, K2tog, K1, K2tog, K2   (18sts)
- 12th row: P
- 13th row: (K2, K2tog)x4, K2   (14sts)
- Work 5 rows SS starting with P
- 19th row: K1, inc in next, K4, inc in next, inc in next, K4, inc in next, K1   (18sts)
- Work 7 rows SS beginning with P
- 27th row: K1, sl1, K1, psso, K12, K2tog, K1   (16sts)
- 28th row: P1, P2tog, P10, P2tog, P1   (14sts)
- 29th row: K1, sl1, K1, psso, K8, K2tog, K1   (12sts)
- 30th row: P
- Cast off

To make up: Join front to back. Stuff.

ARMS – MAKE TWO

COLOUR 1
- Size 13/3.25mm needles

- WORKING FROM SHOULDER TO WRIST
- Cast on 5
- 1st row: K
- 2nd row: P
- 3rd row: K row – inc in 1st & last   (7sts)
- 4th row: P
- 5th row: K row – inc in 1st & last   (9sts)
- 6th row: P
- Work 24 rows

TO CREATE LEFT HAND
- 31st row: K2, put 2 on pin, K5
- 32nd row: P to end bringing 2 sections together   (7sts)

- 33rd row: K
- 34th row: P
- 35th row: K2tog, K2tog, K2tog, K1
- 36th row: P2tog, P2tog
- Pull thread through

TO CREATE RIGHT HAND
- 31st row: K5, put 2 on pin, K2   (7sts)
- 32nd row: P
- 33rd row: K
- 34th row: P
- 35th row: K1, K2tog, K2tog, K2tog
- 36th row: P2tog, P2tog
- Pull thread through

THUMB – SAME FOR BOTH HANDS
- Put 2sts from pin on double-ended needle
- Join thread, K2
- K2tog as i-cord
- Pull thread through

To make up: Join seams. Stuff. Add to body.

BOOTS AND LEGS – MAKE TWO

COLOUR 2
- Size 10/3.25mm needles

- Cast on 24
- 1st row: K
- 2nd row: P
- 3rd row: K10, K2tog, K2tog, K10   (22sts)
- 4th row: P10, P2tog, P10   (21sts)
- 5th row: K5, (K2tog, K1)x3, K2tog, K5   (17sts)
- 6th row: P
- 7th row: K4, cast off 9, K3   (8sts)
- 8th row: P, pulling 2 sections of 4sts together

- Work 4 rows SS starting with K
- 13th row: K1, inc in next, K4, inc in next, K1   (10sts)
- 14th row: P
- Break wool, JOIN COLOUR 1
- Work 6 rows SS starting with K
- 21st row: K1, inc in next, K6, inc in next, K1   (12sts)
- Work 21 rows SS starting with P
- Cast off

CREATING HEEL OF BOOT
- Stitch back seam of boots
- Pick-up 8 stitches along heel edge of boot from right to left – RS facing. Turn –
- 1st row: Cast on 1, P9
- 2nd row: Cast on 1, K10
- 3rd row: P1, (P2tog)x4, P1   (6sts)
- 4th row: K1, K2tog, K2tog, K1   (4sts)
- Cast off

To make up: Sew-up sole of boot and heel – stuff boot. Join leg seam & stuff. Wet boot with warm water, squeeze, shape and dry.

*Tip: Stuff boots with offcuts of black wool rather than white wadding, which tends to show through.

HEAD
COLOUR 1
- Size 10/3.25mm needles

HEAD – FRONT
- Cast on 6
- 1st row: K
- 2nd row: P
- 3rd row: K row – inc in 1st & last (8sts)
- 4th row: P
- 5th row: K row – inc in 1st & last (10sts)

- 6th row: P
- 7th row: K row – inc in 1st & last (12sts)
- 8th row: P
- 9th row: K row – inc in 1st & last (14sts)
- Work 7 rows SS starting with P
- 17th row: K1, sl1, K1, psso, K8, K2tog, K1   (12sts)
- 18th row: P
- 19th row: K1, sl1, K1, psso, K6, K2tog, K1   (10sts)
- 20th row: P
- Cast off

HEAD – BACK
- Cast on 6
- 1st row: K
- 2nd row: P
- 3rd row: K row – inc in 1st and last (8sts)
- 4th row: P
- 5th row: Inc in 1st, K2, K2tog, K2, inc in last   (9sts)
- 6th row: P
- CHANGE TO COLOUR 6
- 7th row: Inc in 1st, K3, inc in next, K3, inc in last   (12sts)
- 8th row: P
- 9th row: Inc in 1st, K4, inc in next, inc in next, K4, inc in last   (16sts)
- Work 5 rows SS starting with P
- 15th row: K5, K2tog, K2, K2tog, K5 (14sts)
- 16th row: P
- 17th row: K1, sl1, K1, psso, K8, K2tog, K1   (12sts)
- 18th row: P
- 19th row: K1, sl1, K1, psso, K6, K2tog, K1   (10sts)
- 20th row: P
- Cast off

To make up: Join front and back. Stuff. Attach all parts to body.

SHIRT FRONT
WORKING FROM HIP TO SHOULDER
COLOUR 5
- Size 13/2.25mm needles

- Cast on 24
- Work 22 rows SS starting with K
- 23rd row: K row – inc in 1st and last (26sts)
- Work 12 rows SS starting with P
- Cast off

To make up: Stitch onto body front at shoulders and hips. Add 3 to 4 small white beads for buttons.

COLLAR
COLOUR 5
- Size 13/2.25mm needles

- Cast on 26
- Work 8 rows SS starting with K
- Cast off

To make up: Fold and iron under a damp cloth. Attach around neck and to shirt front.

TROUSERS
COLOUR 3
- Size 13/2.25mm needles

- Cast on 24
- Work 38 rows SS starting with K
- 39th row: K1, inc in next, K20, inc in next, K1   (26sts)
- Work 9 rows SS starting with P
- 49th row: K1, inc in next, K22, inc in next, K1   (28sts)
- 50th row: P
- 51st row: K1, inc in next, K24, inc in next, K1   (30sts)
- 52nd row: P

- 53rd row: Cast off 2, K27   (28sts)
- 54th row: Cast off 2, P25   (26sts)
- Work 12 rows SS starting with K
- CHANGE TO COLOUR 4 FOR BELT DETAIL
- 67th row: K
- 68th row: P
- CHANGE TO COLOUR 3
- 69th row: K
- 70th row: P
- Cast off

Repeat rows 1 to 70 for second leg.

To make up: Join inside leg seams. Join crotch. Dress doll.

JACKET
COLOUR 3
- Size 13/2.25mm needles

- Cast on 50
- 1st row: P
- 2nd row: Inc in 1st, K48, inc in last (52sts)
- 3rd row: Inc in 1st, P50, inc in last (54sts)
- 4th row: Inc in 1st, K52, inc in last (56sts)
- Work 7 rows SS starting with P

FOR TOP EDGES OF POCKET FLAPS:
- 12th row: K5 in COLOUR 3, K9 in COLOUR 4, K28 in COLOUR 3, K9 in COLOUR 4, K5 in COLOUR 3
- 13th row: P5 in COLOUR 3, P9 in COLOUR 4, P28 in COLOUR 3, P9 in COLOUR 4, P5 in COLOUR 3
- CONTINUE IN COLOUR 3
- 14th row: K
- 15th row: P
- 16th row: K14, K2tog, K24, K2tog, K14 (54sts)
- Work 19 rows SS starting with P

WORKING ON FRONT RIGHT – SPLITTING OFF FOR ARMHOLES
- 36th row: K13, K2tog   (14sts)
- Put remaining sts on pin
- 37th row: P2tog, P12   (13sts)
- Work 6 rows SS starting with K
- 44th row: Cast off 5, K7   (8sts)
- 45th row: P
- 46th row: K2tog, K6   (7sts)
- 47th row: Cast off 3, P3   (4sts)
- 48th row: K2tog, K2   (3sts)
- Cast off

WORKING ON LEFT FRONT – RS FACING
- Put 15sts on needle – hold remaining sts on pin
- 36th row: P13, P2tog   (14sts)
- 37th row: K2tog, K12   (13sts)
- Work 6 rows SS starting with P
- 44th row: Cast off 5, P7   (8sts)
- 45th row: K
- 46th row: P2tog, P6   (7sts)
- 47th row: Cast off 3, K3   (4sts)
- 48th row: P2tog, P2   (3sts)
- Cast off

WORKING ON JACKET BACK ON REMAINING 24STS
RS FACING
- 36th row: K2tog, K20, K2tog   (22sts)
- Work 3 rows SS starting with P
- 40th row: K row – inc in 1st and last (24sts)
- Work 7 rows SS starting with P
- Cast off

To make up: Join shoulder seams.

JACKET SLEEVES
COLOUR 5
- Size 13/2.25mm needles

- Cast on 20

- 1st row: K
- 2nd row: P
- CHANGE TO COLOUR 3
- Work 34 rows SS starting with K
- 37th row: Cast off 4, K15   (16sts)
- 38th row: Cast off 4, P11   (12sts)
- 39th row: K2tog, K8, K2tog   (10sts)
- Work 3 rows SS starting with P
- 43rd row: K2tog, K2tog, K2, K2tog, K2tog   (6sts)
- 44th row: P2tog, P2, P2tog   (4sts)
- Cast off

To make up: Join seams. Inset in jacket. Dress Doll. Add beads for buttons on jacket front.

TIE
COLOUR 4
- Size 14/2.00mm needles

- Cast on 3
- Work 24 rows SS starting with K
- 25th row: K1, inc in next, K1   (4sts)
- Work 43 rows SS starting with P
- 69th row: K2tog, K2tog   (2sts)
- 70th row: K2tog – pull wool through

To make up: Steam press flat. Fold in half making a knot and stitch in place around neck.

HAIR

Use photographs to reference the slight differences in the hairstyles. Cut lengths of COLOUR 6. Separate strands and press flat with a steam iron. Thread a darning needle with 3 or 4 strands at a time and overlay long stitches from crown to nape of neck, using the coloured back of head as a guideline, and in loops or loose lengths for fringes.

*Tip: Make over-long and trim when fringe looks thick enough.

TO CREATE FACE

Add beads for eyes. The nose and ears are fashioned from crocheted chains of the flesh-coloured wool. Pin and stitch on when you feel you have a good likeness. Add eyebrows and mouth.

You will need

MATERIALS:
Colour Codes:
1 Rowan Baby Merino Silk DK
(Shade SH674 – Shell Pink) – For Body
2 Debbie Bliss Rialto 4-Ply
(Shade 22003 – Black) – For Tuxedo,
Trousers, Shoes and Hair
3 John Lewis Baby 4-Ply (White) –
For Shirt Front and Cuffs

Black embroidery thread
Small piece of black Petersham
for bowtie
Small beads for buttons of jacket
and shirt front
Black millinery wire
Small piece buckram
Small piece of narrow plastic tubing or
drinking straw
Yarn for creating facial features
Metallic grey craft paint
Jewellery pliers
Stuffing

NEEDLES:
Size 10/3.25mm
Size 10/3.25mm double-ended
Crochet hook – 4.00mm
Darning needle

James Bond

When Ian Fleming created his fictional hero, he could not possibly have known what he was starting. He named him after an American ornithologist who, according to Fleming, had the sort of dull but manly name he was looking for. He wanted Bond to be neutral, a 'blunt instrument' who would be the rock in the story as the action unfolded around him. Inspired by Fleming's own wartime experiences in Naval Intelligence, James Bond was the distilled essence of the wartime agents and heroes he had worked with, along with a decent smattering of his own likes and dislikes. And when he set out to write 'the spy story to end all spy stories', James Bond was born.

Ian Fleming was from a wealthy background, educated at Eton and Sandhurst, the son of an MP and grandson of banker Robert Fleming. The war changed his life, however, as he oversaw various commando operations and took on a key role before the Normandy landings in 1944. Later, when Fleming wrote his first book, it was his brother Peter who persuaded a publisher to take on Ian's books, and they were an instant success that just kept on building. He also wrote the hugely successful children's book *Chitty-Chitty-Bang-Bang*, based on a story he told to his son Caspar.

Fleming was a heavy smoker and drinker, which led to various health problems, and the staggering global success of the shaken not stirred James Bond franchise and the movies that followed happened largely after Fleming's death in 1964 at the age of fifty-six. It is now, of course, a billion dollar industry, all based on the quintessentially British 007 and his licence to kill.

BODY – FRONT

COLOUR I

- Size 10/3.25mm needles

- Cast on 14
- 1st row: K
- 2nd row: P
- 3rd row: K1, inc in next, K10, inc in next, K1 (16sts)
- Work 3 rows SS starting with P
- 7th row: K1, K2tog, K2, K2tog, K2, K2tog, K2, K2tog, K1 (12sts)
- Work 5 rows SS starting with P
- 13th row: K2, inc in next, K6, inc in next, K2 (14sts)
- 14th row: P
- 15th row: Inc in 1st, K3, inc in next, K4, inc in next, K3, inc in last (18sts)
- 16th row: P
- 17th row: K5, inc in next, K6, inc in next, K5 (20sts)
- Work 3 rows SS starting with P
- 21st row: K1, sl1, K1, psso, K14, K2tog, K1 (18sts)
- Work 5 rows SS starting with P
- 27th row: K1, sl1, K1, psso, K12, K2tog, K1 (16sts)
- 28th row: P1, P2tog, P10, P2tog, P1 (14sts)
- 29th row: K
- 30th row: P
- Cast off

BODY – BACK

COLOUR I

- Size 10/3.25mm needles

- Cast on 14
- 1st row: K
- 2nd row: P
- 3rd row: K2, inc in next, K1, inc in next, K4, inc in next, K1, inc in next, K2 (18sts)

- 4th row: P
- 5th row: K3, inc in next, K1, inc in next, K6, inc in next, K1, inc in next, K3 (22sts)
- Work 3 rows SS starting with P
- 9th row: K1, K2tog, K16, K2tog, K1 (20sts)
- 10th row: P
- 11th row: K2, K2tog, K1, K2tog, K6, K2tog, K1, K2tog, K2 (16sts)
- 12th row: P
- 13th row: K2, K2tog, K2, K2tog, K2tog, K2, K2tog, K2 (12sts)
- Work 4 rows SS starting with P
- 18th row: P3, inc in next, P4, inc in next, P3 (14sts)
- 19th row: K1, inc in next, K4, inc in next, inc in next, K4, inc in next, K1 (18sts)
- Work 9 rows SS starting with P
- 29th row: K1, sl1, K1, psso, K12, K2tog, K1 (16sts).
- 30th row: P1, P2tog, P10, P2tog, P1 (14sts)
- 31st row: K1, sl1, K1, psso, K8, K2tog, K1 (12sts)
- 32nd row: P
- Cast off

To make up: Join front to back. Stuff.

HEAD – FRONT

COLOUR I

- Size 10/3.25mm needles

- Cast on 6
- 1st row: K
- 2nd row: P
- 3rd row: K row – inc in 1st & last (8sts)
- 4th row: P
- 5th row: K row – inc in 1st & last (10sts)
- 6th row: P

- 7th row: K row – inc in 1st & last (12sts)
- 8th row: P
- 9th row: K row – inc in 1st & last (14sts)
- Work 7 rows SS starting with P
- 17th row: K1, sl1, K1, psso, K8, K2tog, K1 (12sts)
- 18th row: P
- 19th row: K1, sl1, K1, psso, K6, K2tog, K1 (10sts)
- 20th row: P
- Cast off

HEAD – BACK

COLOUR I

- Cast on 6
- 1st row: K
- 2nd row: P
- 3rd row: K row – inc in 1st and last (8sts)
- 4th row: P
- 5th row: K row – inc in 1st and last (10sts)
- 6th row: P
- 7th row: K row – inc in 1st, K2, inc in next, K2, inc in next, K2, inc in last (14sts)
- 8th row: P
- 9th row: K row – inc in 1st and last (16sts)
- Work 3 rows SS starting with P
- 13th row: K2, inc in next, K2, inc in next, K1, inc in next, inc in next, K1, inc in next, K2, inc in next, K2 (22sts)
- Work 3 rows SS starting with P
- 17th row: K1, (K2tog, K2)x2, K2tog, K2tog, (K2, K2tog)x2, K1 (16sts)
- 18th row: P
- 19th row: K2 K2tog K1, K2tog, K2, K2tog, K1, K2tog, K2 (12sts)
- 20th row: P3, P2tog, P2, P2tog, P3

(10sts)
- Cast off

To make up: Join front and back together. Stuff.

ARMS – MAKE TWO
COLOUR 1
- Size 10/3.25mm needles

- WORKING FROM SHOULDER TO WRIST
- Cast on 5
- 1st row: K
- 2nd row: P
- 3rd row: K row – inc in 1st & last (7sts)
- 4th row: P
- 5th row: K row – inc in 1st & last (9sts)
- 6th row: P
- Work 24 rows SS starting with K

TO CREATE LEFT HAND
- 31st row: K2, put 2 on pin, K5
- 32nd row: P to end bringing 2 sections together   (7sts)
- 33rd row: K
- 34th row: P
- 35th row: K2tog, K2tog, K2tog, K1
- 36th row: P2tog, P2tog
- Pull thread through

TO CREATE RIGHT HAND
- 31st row: K5, put 2 on pin, K2   (7sts)
- 32nd row: P
- 33rd row: K
- 34th row: P
- 35th row: K1, K2tog, K2tog, K2tog
- 36th row: P2tog, P2tog
- Pull thread through

THUMB – SAME FOR BOTH HANDS
COLOUR 1
- Put 2sts from pin on double-ended needle
- Join thread, K2
- K2tog as i-cord
- Pull thread through

To make up: Join seams. Stuff. Add to body.

LEGS – MAKE TWO
COLOUR 2
- Size 10/3.25mm needles

- Cast on 24
- 1st row: K
- 2nd row: P
- 3rd row: K10, K2tog, K2tog, K10 (22sts)
- 4th row: P10. P2tog, P10 (21sts)
- 5th row: K5, (K2tog, K1)x3, K2tog, K5 (17sts)
- 6th row: P
- 7th row: K4, cast off 9, K3   (8sts)
- 8th row: P, pulling 2 sections of 4 together
- Work 4 rows SS starting with K
- 13th row: K1, inc in next, K4, inc in next, K1   (10sts)
- 14th row: P
- CHANGE TO COLOUR 1
- Work 6 rows SS starting with K
- 21st row: K1, inc in next, K6, inc in next, K1   (12sts)
- Work 7 rows SS starting with P
- 29th row: K1, inc in next, K8, inc in next, K1   (14sts)
- Work 18 rows SS starting with P
- Cast off

To make up: Sew-up foot. Stuff with offcuts of black wool rather than white wadding, which tends to show through. Join leg seams. Stuff with wadding. Use black embroidery thread for shoelaces.

SHIRT FRONT
COLOUR 3
- Size 10/3.25mm needles

- Cast on 16
- Work 24 rows SS starting with P
- 25th row: P8, turn –
- Now working on these 8sts:
- 26th row: Cast off 2, K5 (6sts)
- 27th row: P6
- 28th row: K2tog, K4 (5sts)
- 29th row: P5
- Cast off

- Join wool at centre neck
- 26th row: Cast off 2, P5
- 27th row: K
- 28th row: P2tog, P4 (5sts)
- 29th row: K
- Cast off
-
- To make up: Attach to body at shoulders and hips.

COLLAR
- Cast on 20
- Work 5 rows SS starting with P
- Cast off

To make up: Fold and press. Attach around neck. Catch at centre-front to shirt front.

TUXEDO
COLOUR 2
- Size 10/3.25mm double-ended needles

BACK
- Cast on 16
- Work 12 rows SS starting with K
- 13th row: K1, K2tog, K10, K2tog, K1 (14sts)
- 14th row: P
- Set aside on pin

FRONT LEFT
- Cast on 17
- 1st row: K
- 2nd row: P
- 3rd row: K15, inc in next, K1 (18sts)
- 4th row: P
- 5th row: K6, K2tog, K8, inc in next, K1
- 6th row: P
- 7th row: K6, K2tog, K8, inc in next, K1 (18sts)
- 8th row: P
- 9th row: K6, K2tog, K8, inc in next, K1 (18sts)
- 10th row: P
- 11th row: K15, K2tog, K1 (17sts)
- 12th row: P7, K5, P5 (to mark top of pocket)
- 13th row: K
- 14th row: P

FRONT RIGHT
- Cast on 17
- 1st row: K
- 2nd row: P
- 3rd row: K1, inc in next, K15 (18sts)
- 4th row: P
- 5th row: K1, inc in next, K8, K2tog, K6 (18sts)
- 6th row: P
- 7th row: K1, inc in next, K8, K2tog, K6 (18sts)
- 8th row: P
- 9th row: K1, inc in next, K8, K2tog, K6 (18sts)
- 10th row: P
- 11th row: K1, K2tog, K15 (17sts)

- 12th row: P5, K5, P7 (to mark top of pocket)
- 13th row: K
- 14th row: P

To form the two vents in the jacket with the back overlapping the two front pieces: Working onto left-hand needle, with RS facing, slip 15sts of front left, 1st of back, 16th of front left, 2nd of back, 17th of front left, 10sts of back, 1st of front right, 13th of back, 2nd of front right, 14th of back, 15sts of front right (48sts)

- 15th row: K15, K2tog, K2tog, K10, K2tog, K2tog, K15 (44sts)
- 16th row: P4, P2tog, P5, P2tog, P6, P2tog, P2, P2tog, P6, P2tog, P5, P2tog, P4 (38sts)
- 17th row: K
- 18th row: P
- 19th row: K1, inc in next, K34, inc in next, K1 (40sts)
- 20th row: P
- 21st row: K1, inc in next, K36, inc in next, K1 (42sts)
- 22nd row: P5, inc in next, P6, inc in next, P4, P2tog, P4, P2tog, P4, inc in next, P6, inc in next, P5 (44sts)
- Work 8 rows SS starting with K

TO CREATE RIGHT-SIDE FRONT
- 31st row: K12, turn – Put remaining sts on pin
- Work 10 rows SS starting with P
- 42nd row: Cast off 6, P5 (6sts)
- Work 3 rows SS starting with K
- 46th row: P4, P2tog
- 47th row: K4, turn, P4
- 48th row: K5
- 49th row: P5
- Cast off

TO CREATE LEFT-SIDE FRONT – WS FACING – Remaining 12sts
- 31st row: P6, K4, P2
- Work 10 rows SS starting with K
- 42nd row: Cast off 6, K5 (6sts)
- Work 3 rows SS starting with P
- 46th row: K4, K2tog
- 47th row: P4, turn, K4
- 48th row: P5
- 49th row: K5
- Cast off

TO CREATE BACK – RS FACING – next 20sts. Hold remaining sts on pin.
- 31st row: K2tog, K17, K2tog (19sts)
- Work 7 rows SS starting with P
- 39th row: Cast off 3, K15 (16sts)
- 40th row: Cast off 3, P12 (13sts)
- 41st row: K2tog, K9, K2tog (11sts)
- 42nd row: Cast off 2, P8
- 43rd row: Cast off 2, K7
- Cast off

To make up: Join shoulder seams. Turn back the shawl collar and press flat. Join collar centre back and attach to jacket at neck edge.

JACKET SLEEVES – MAKE TWO

COLOUR 3
- Size 10/3.25mm needles

- Cast on 15
- 1st row: P
- CHANGE TO COLOUR 2
- 2nd row: K
- Work 13 rows SS starting with P
- 16th row: K1, inc in next, K11, inc in next, K1 (17sts)
- Work 10 rows SS starting with P
- 27th row: Cast off 3, P13 (14sts)
- 28th row: Cast off 3, K10 (11sts)
- 29th row: Cast off 3, P7 (8sts)

- 30th row: Cast off 3, K4 (5sts)
- Cast off

To make up: Sew seams. Inset into jacket.

TROUSERS
COLOUR 2
- Size 10/3.25mm needles

TO CREATE FIRST LEG
- Cast on 22
- 1st row: K
- 2nd row: P
- 3rd row: K1, K2tog, K16, K2tog, K1 (20sts)
- Work 48 rows SS starting with P
- 52nd row: Cast off 2, K to end (18sts)
- 53rd row: Cast off 2, P to end (16sts)
- 54th row: K
- Put on pin

Repeat rows 1 to 54 to create second leg.

KNITTING LEGS TOGETHER
- Slip both legs onto left-hand needle, RS facing –
- 55th row: K15, K2tog, K15 (31sts)
- Work 6 rows SS starting with P
- 62nd row: K6, K2tog, K15, K2tog, K6 (29sts)
- 63rd row: P
- 64th row: K
- 65th row: P
- Cast off

To make up: Join leg and crotch seams. Attach to doll.

BOW TIE
Cut small piece of black Petersham ribbon, fold and fashion into bow tie shape. Stitch at neck.

HAIR
COLOUR 2
- Size 10/3.25mm needles

- Cast on 12
- 1st row: K
- 2nd row: P
- 3rd row: K2, inc in next, K6, inc in next, K2 (14sts)
- 4th row: P4, inc in next, P4, inc in next, P4 (16sts)
- 5th row: K1, inc in next, K2, inc in next, K6, inc in next, K2, inc in next, K1 (20sts)
- Work 3 rows SS starting with P
- 9th row: K1, inc in next, K3, K2tog, K6, K2tog, K3, inc in next, K1 (20sts)
- 10th row: Cast on 3, P to end (23sts)
- 11th row: Cast on 3, K to end (26sts)
- 12th row: P2, P2tog, P4, P2tog, P6, P2tog, P4, P2tog, P2 (22sts)
- 13th row: K1, K2tog, K16, K2tog, K1 (20sts)
- 14th row: Cast off 2, P17 (18sts)
- 15th row: Cast off 2, K15 (16sts)
- 16th row: P2, P2tog, P2, P2tog, P2tog, P2, P2tog, P2 (12sts)
- 17th row: Cast off 2, K9 (10sts)
- 18th row: Cast off 2, P7 (8sts)
- 19th row: K8
- 20th row: P1, P2tog, P2, P2tog, P1 (6sts)
- 21st row: K1, K2tog, K2tog, K1 (4sts)
- 22nd row: P2tog, P2tog (2sts)
- Cast off

To make up: Using photo reference, sew hair to head after positioning ears. Lift hair at centre front by tucking a small piece of wadding under hairline. Using black embroidery thread, add a few long stitches from front to back to give a combed-back 'Brylcreem' look.

TO CREATE FACE
The nose and ears are crocheted chains in flesh colour, stitched to head and face. Use own choice of wool for eyes, brows and mouth.

GUN
Find a photo reference for this model. Use jewellery pliers to create a skeleton shape of the gun from millinery wire. Feed two lengths of plastic tube onto the wire to create the barrel and magazine profiles. Stitch or glue a small piece of buckram to the handgrip. Paint in gun metal grey.

MATERIALS:
Colour Codes:
1 MillaMia Sweden Naturally Soft
Merino (Shade 122 – Petal)
2 Rowan Panama
(Shade 00309 – Blue)
3 Rowan Kidsilk Haze (Shade 00592)
4 Debbie Bliss Rialto Lace (Black)
5 Rowan Creative Focus Worsted
(Shade 02132)

Beads for jacket buttons and white
beads for pearl earrings and necklace
8 gold bugle beads for bag
Yarn for creating facial features
Small piece of card for gusset of bag
Sequin shape and silver beads
for brooch
Stuffing

NEEDLES:
Size 11/3.00mm
Size 10/3.25mm double-ended
Size 13/2.25mm
Crochet hook 4.00mm
Darning needle

Margaret Thatcher

Love her or hate her, you could never ignore her. Margaret Hilda Roberts was born in Grantham in 1925, the daughter of grocer Alfred Roberts, who served as Mayor and was active in local politics. The young Margaret was studious and read Chemistry at Oxford University whilst taking a keen interest in politics. She so impressed the Conservative Association in Dartford, Kent, that they invited her to become their candidate in the forthcoming General Election. She narrowly missed overturning the Labour majority, however, then took a break as she studied for the bar and had her children.

Returning to politics, she was elected Member of Parliament for Finchley in 1959, rising to become Education Secretary in 1970. Then, as Edward Heath's leadership faltered, Margaret Thatcher seized her opportunity and was elected leader of the Conservative Party. Four years later, Britain had its first woman Prime Minister who would dominate the political scene for the next decade and more. Married to wealthy businessman Denis Thatcher, Margaret was reinvented as a woman of the people who was strong on monetarist economic theory and tough on the unions. She championed privatisation and the free market, home ownership and the special relationship with the United States. Her defining moments were the Falklands War and the miners' strike, both of which remain controversial to some to this day. After a tumultuous tenure lasting three terms and eleven years, Margaret Thatcher was replaced as leader of her party in a somewhat abrupt manner by John Major, an altogether different sort, and she famously left Downing Street in tears.

The reaction to the news of her death in April 2013 was as sharply divided as ever but there can be no doubt that, whether you agreed with her or not, Margaret Thatcher was British to the core and was a political force to be reckoned with.

BODY

COLOUR 1
- Size 11/3.00mm needles

BODY – FRONT
- Cast on 16
- 1st row: K
- 2nd row: P
- 3rd row: K1, inc in next, K12 inc in next, K1   (18sts)
- Work 3 rows SS starting with P
- 7th row: K1, K2tog, K2, K2tog, K4, K2tog, K2, K2tog, K1   (14sts)
- Work 3 rows SS starting with P
- 11th row: K2, inc in next, K8, inc in next, K2   (16sts)
- 12th row: P
- 13th row: K row – inc in 1st, K3, inc in next, K6, inc in next, K3, inc in last   (20sts)
- Work 5 rows SS starting with P
- 19th row: K1, sl1, K1, psso, inc in next, K12, inc in next, K2tog, K1   (20sts)
- Work 3 rows SS starting with P
- 23rd row: K1, sl1, K1, psso, inc in next, K12, inc in next, K2tog, K1   (20sts)
- 24th row: P1, inc in next, P16, inc in next, P1   (22sts)
- 25th row: K1, sl1, K1, psso, inc in next, K14, inc in next, K2tog, K1   (22sts)
- 26th row: P1, inc in next, P18, inc in next, P1   (24sts)
- 27th row: K1, sl1, K1 psso, K18, K2tog, K1   (22sts)
- Cast off

BODY – BACK
- Cast on 16
- 1st row: K
- 2nd row: P
- 3rd row: K2, inc in next, K1, inc in next, K6, inc in next, K1, inc in next, K2   (20sts)
- 4th row: P

- 5th row: K3, inc in next, K1, inc in next, K8, inc in next, K1, inc in next, K3   (24sts)
- Work 3 rows SS starting with P
- 9th row: K1, K2tog, K18, K2tog, K1   (22sts)
- 10th row: P
- 11th row: K2, K2tog, K1, K2tog, K8, K2tog, K1, K2tog, K2   (18sts)
- 12th row: P
- 13th row: K2, K2tog, K2, K2tog, K2, K2tog, K2, K2tog, K2   (14sts)
- Work 5 rows SS starting with P
- 19th row: K1, inc in next, K4, inc in next, inc in next, K4, inc in next, K1   (18sts)
- 20th row: P
- 21st row: K1, inc in next, K14, inc in next, K1   (20sts)
- 22nd row: P
- 23rd row: K1, inc in next, K16, inc in next, K1   (22sts)
- 24th row: P
- 25th row: K1, inc in next, K18, inc in next, K1   (24sts)
- 26th row: P
- 27th row: K1, sl1, K1, psso, inc in next, K16, inc in next, K2tog, K1   (24sts)
- 28th row: P
- 29th row: K
- Cast off

To make up: Join two pieces together. Stuff – do not overstuff.

UPPER TORSO/BUST

(HORIZONTAL TRIANGULAR PRISM SHAPE) – MAKE TWO SMALL TRIANGLES
COLOUR 1
- Size 11/3.00mm needles

- Cast on 10
- 1st row: K

- 2nd row: P2tog, P6, P2tog   (8sts)
- 3rd row: K2tog, K4, K2tog   (6sts)
- 4th row: P2tog, P2, P2tog   (4sts)
- 5th row: K2tog, K2tog   (2sts)
- 6th row: K2tog – pull wool through
- Set aside
- The cast-on edge is the base of the triangles

CENTRAL BUST PANEL – MAKE ONE
COLOUR 1
- Size 11/3.00mm needles

- Cast on 14
- 1st row: K
- 2nd row: P
- 3rd row: K2tog, K10, K2tog   (12sts)
- 4th row: P
- 5th row: K2tog, K8, K2tog   (10sts)
- 6th row: P
- 7th row: K2tog, K6, K2tog   (8sts)
- 8th row: P
- 9th row: K
- 10th row: P row – inc in 1st and last   (10sts)
- 11th row: K
- 12th row: P row – inc in 1st and last   (12sts)
- 13th row: K
- 14th row: P row – inc in 1st and last   (14sts)
- 15th row: K
- Cast off

To make up: Stitch a triangle either end of the central bust panel to form a 'roof' shape. Attach to upper torso of body shape, leaving a small gap to push stuffing through. When happy with shape, sew-up the gap.

ARMS –MAKE TWO

COLOUR 1
- Size 11/3.00mm needles

- WORKING FROM SHOULDER TO WRIST
- Cast on 5
- 1st row: K
- 2nd row: P
- 3rd row: K row – inc in 1st & last (7sts)
- 4th row: P
- 5th row: K row – inc in 1st & last (9sts)
- 6th row: P
- Work 24 rows

TO CREATE LEFT HAND
- 31st row: K2, put 2 on pin, K5
- 32nd row: P to end bringing 2 sections together (7sts)
- 33rd row: K
- 34th row: P
- 35th row: K2tog, K2tog, K2tog, K1
- 36th row: P2tog, P2tog
- Pull thread through

TO CREATE RIGHT HAND
- 31st row: K5, put 2 on pin, K2 (7sts)
- 32nd row: P
- 33rd row: K
- 34th row: P
- 35th row: K1, K2tog, K2tog, K2tog
- 36th row: P2tog, P2tog
- Pull thread through

THUMB – SAME FOR BOTH HANDS
- Put 2sts from pin on double-ended needle
- Join thread, K2
- K2tog as i-cord
- Pull thread through

To make up: Join seams. Stuff. Attach to body.

LEGS – MAKE TWO
COLOUR 1
- Size 11/3.00mm needles

- Cast on 20
- 1st row: K7, K2tog, K2, K2tog, K7 (18sts)
- 2nd row: P8, P2tog, P8 (17sts)
- 3rd row: K
- 4th row: Left leg: P2tog, P6, P2tog, P5, P2tog (14sts)
- Right leg: P2tog, P5, P2tog, P6, P2tog (14sts)
- 5th row: K14
- 6th row: P3, cast off 8, P2 (6sts)
- 7th row: K across the 6sts, drawing them together
- Work 5 rows SS starting with P
- 13th row: K1, inc in next, K2, inc in next, K1 (8sts)
- 14th row: P
- 15th row: K1, inc in next, K4, inc in next, K1 (10sts)
- 16th row: P
- 17th row: K1, inc in next, K6, inc in next, K1 (12sts)
- 18th row: P
- 19th row: K1, inc in next, K8, inc in next, K1 (14sts)
- Work 5 rows SS starting with P
- 25th row: K1, sl1, K1, psso, K8, K2tog, K1
- 26th row: P1, P2tog, P6, P2tog, P1 (10sts)
- Work 4 rows SS starting with K
- 31st row: K1, inc in next, K6, inc in next, K1 (12sts)
- Work 7 rows SS starting with P
- 39th row: K1, inc in next, K8, inc in next, K1 (14sts)
- Work 7 rows SS starting with P
- 47th row: K1, inc in next, K10, inc in next, K1 (16sts)
- 48th row: P

- 49th row: K
- Cast off

To make up: Join seams. Stuff. Attach to body.

HEAD
HEAD – FRONT
COLOUR 1
- Size 11/3.00mm needles

RIGHT SIDE OF FACE
- Cast on 3
- 1st row: K
- 2nd row: P
- 3rd row: cast on 2, K5
- 4th row: P row – inc in 1st, P3, inc in last (7sts)
- 5th row: K row – inc in 1st and last (9sts)
- 6th row: P
- Hold these sts on a pin

LEFT SIDE OF FACE
- Cast on 3
- 1st row: K
- 2nd row: P
- 3rd row: K
- 4th row: cast on 2, P5
- 5th row: K row – inc in 1st, K3, inc in last (7sts)
- 6th row: P row – inc in 1st and last (9sts)
- Knit across these 2 pieces to join together –
- 7th row: K8, K2tog, K8 (17sts)
- Work 7 rows SS starting with P
- 15th row: K2tog, K13, K2tog (15sts)
- 16th row: P
- 17th row: K2tog, K11, K2tog (13sts)
- 18th row: P
- 19th row: K2tog, K9, K2tog (11sts)
- 20th row: P
- 21st row: K2tog, K7, K2tog (9sts)
- Cast off

HEAD – BACK

- Cast on 6
- 1st row: K
- 2nd row: P
- 3rd row: K row – inc in 1st and last (8sts)
- 4th row: P
- 5th row: K row – inc in 1st and last (10sts)
- 6th row: P
- 7th row: K row – inc in 1st and last (12sts)
- 8th row: P
- 9th row: K row – inc in 1st and last (14sts)
- Work 8 rows SS starting with P
- 18th row: P2tog, P10, P2tog   (12sts)
- 19th row: K
- 20th row: P2tog, P8, P2tog   (10sts)
- 21st row: K
- Cast off

SUIT SKIRT

COLOUR 2

- Size 11/3.00mm needles

- Cast on 46
- Work 10 rows SS starting with K
- 11th row: Cast off 3, K42   (43sts)
- Work 10 rows SS starting with P
- 22nd row: P10, P2tog, P19, P2tog, P10 (41sts)
- Work 3 rows SS starting with K
- 26th row: P10, P2tog, P17, P2tog, P10 (39sts)
- Work 3 rows SS starting with K
- 30th row: P10, P2tog, P15, P2tog, P10 (37sts)
- Work 3 rows SS starting with K
- 34th row: P10, P2tog, P13, P2tog, P10 (35sts)
- 35th row: K
- 36th row: P
- Cast off

To make up: Press under damp cloth. Join centre seam at back, leaving kick-pleat open.

JACKET

COLOUR 2

- Size 11/3.00mm needles

- Cast on 52
- Work 12 rows SS starting with K
- 13th row: K15, K2tog, K18, K2tog, K15 (50sts)
- 14th row: P49, K1
- 15th row: K
- 16th row: P49, K1
- 17th row: K15, inc in next, K18, inc in next, K15   (52sts)
- 18th row: P51, K1
- 19th row: K
- 20th row: P51, K1
- 21st row: K

START OF ARMHOLES

- Break thread, put first 37sts on pin. Now working on right front 15sts – WS facing
- 22nd row: Cast off 1, P12, K1   (14sts)
- 23rd row: K
- 24th row: Cast off 6, P6, K1   (8sts)
- 25th row: K7, inc in last   (9sts)
- 26th row: P8, K1   (9sts)
- 27th row: K8, inc in last   (10sts)
- 28th row: P9, K1   (10sts)
- 29th row: K9, inc in last   (11sts)
- 30th row: P10, K1   (11sts)
- 31st row: K10, inc in last   (12sts)
- 32nd row: P11, K1   (12sts)
- 33rd row: K
- 34th row: P11, K1   (12sts)
- 35th row: K11, inc in last   (13sts)
- 36th row: P12, K1
- 37th row: Cast off 5, K7   (8sts)
- Cast off

BACK OF JACKET

- Work on next 22sts, RS facing
- Work 3 rows SS starting with K
- 25th row: P row – inc in 1st and last (24sts)
- Work 6 rows SS starting with K
- Cast off

LEFT-FRONT

- Work on last 15sts, RS facing
- 22nd row: Cast off 1, K13   (14sts)
- 23rd row: P
- 24th row: Cast off 6, K7   (8sts)
- 25th row: P7, inc in last   (9sts)
- 26th row: K
- 27th row: P8, inc in last   (10sts)
- 28th row: K
- 29th row: P9, inc in last   (11sts)
- 30th row: K
- 31st row: P10, inc in last   (12sts)
- Work 3 rows SS starting with K
- 35th row: P11, inc in last   (13sts)
- 36th row: K
- 37th row: Cast off 5, P7   (8sts)
- Cast off

To make up: Press under damp cloth. Join shoulder seams and darts of jacket front.

POCKET FLAPS – MAKE TWO

COLOUR 2

- Size 11/3.00mm needles

- Cast on 9
- 1st row: K
- 2nd row: P
- 3rd row: K
- Cast off

To make up: Attach to jacket front at hip level.

SLEEVES – MAKE TWO

COLOUR 2

- Size 11/3.00mm needles

- Cast on 13
- Work 8 rows SS starting with K
- 9th row: Left arm – K1, inc in next, K11   (14sts)
- Right arm – K11, inc in next, K1 (14sts)
- Work 15 rows SS starting with P
- 25th row: Cast off 2, K11   (12sts)
- 26th row: Cast off 2, P9   (10sts)
- 27th row: K
- 28th row: P
- 29th row: K2tog, K6, K2tog   (8sts)
- 30th row: P2tog, P4, P2tog   (8sts)
- 31st row: K2tog, K2tog, K2tog
- Break wool and draw through last 3sts – tie off

To make up: Press under damp cloth.
Join seams. Inset in jacket.
Dress doll in the suit. Add beads as buttons on jacket front.

HANDBAG

COLOUR 4 – USE DOUBLE

- Size 11/3.00mm needles

- Cast on 14
- Work 4 rows SS starting with K
- 5th row: Cast on 3 – P3, K14   (17sts)
- 6th row: Cast on 3 – K3, P14, K3 (20sts)
- 7th row: P3, K14, P3
- 8th row: K3, P14, K3
- 9th row: P3, K14, P3
- 10th row: K3, P14, K3
- 11th row: P3, K14, P3
- 12th row: K3, P14, K3
- 13th row: P3, K14, P3
- 14th row: K

- 15th row: P3, K14, P3
- 16th row: K3, P14, K3
- 17th row: P3, K14, P3
- 18th row: K3, P14, K3
- 19th row: P
- 20th row: K3, P14, K3
- 21st row: P3, K14, P3
- 22nd row: K3, P14, K3
- 23rd row: P3, K14, P3
- 24th row: K3, P14, K3
- 25th row: P3, K14, P3
- 26th row: K3, P14, K3
- 27th row: Cast off 3, P13, K3   (17sts)
- 28th row: Cast off 3, K13   (14sts)
- Work 4 rows SS starting with P
- Cast off

To make up: Fold in sides and iron under damp cloth. Working inside out join side seams. Cut small piece of card and fit into bottom of bag to hold shape.

TO MAKE HANDLES

- Size 10/3.25mm double-ended needles
- Make two 10cm i-cords using the wool tripled.
- Attach both sides to outside of bag and decorate with gold bugle beads.

SHOES – MAKE TWO

COLOUR 4

- Size 13/2.25mm needles

- Cast on 16
- 1st row: K10, turn –
- 2nd row: P8, turn –
- 3rd row: K14
- 4th row: P2tog, P14   (15sts)
- 5th row: sl3, K7, turn –
- 6th row: P7, turn –
- 7th row: K12   (15sts)
- 8th row: P7, turn –
- 9th row: K7

- 10th row: Cast off 10, P4   (5sts)
- 11th row: K5
- 12th row: P3, turn –
- 13th row: K3, cast on 10
- 14th row: P12, turn –
- 15th row: K12
- 16th row: P15
- 17th row: sl3, K7, turn –
- 18th row: P7, turn –
- 19th row: K11, inc in next   (13sts)
- 20th row: P16
- 21st row: K16
- Cast off

To make up: Press flat under damp cloth. Fold and working inside out stitch back seam of shoe and continue stitching along base. At toe, turn shoe right-side out and make 1 or 2 finishing stitches at pointed toe.

Place on foot – a catching stitch will ensure it stays on.

For heel: Use wool doubled and with darning needle work a heel shape by sewing a few stitches one way then the other to build up a good heel shape. Finish off.

PUSSYCAT BOW

COLOUR 3

- Size 11/3.00mm needles
- Cast on 10
- 1st row: K
- 2nd row: P
- 3rd row: K
- 4th row: P1, P2tog, P4, P2tog, P1 (8sts)
- 5th row: K
- 6th row: P1, P2tog, P2, P2tog, P1 (6sts)
- Work 6 rows SS starting with K
- 13th row: K1, inc in next, K2, inc in next, K1   (8sts)

- Work 5 rows SS starting with P
- 19th row: K1, inc in next, K4, inc in next, K1 (10sts)
- Work 4 rows SS starting with P
- 24th row: K1, inc in next, K6, inc in next, K1 (12sts)
- Work 7 rows SS starting with P
- 32nd row: K1, K2tog, K6, K2tog, K1 (10sts)
- Work 5 rows SS starting with P
- 38th row: K1, K2tog, K4, K2tog, K1 (8sts)
- Work 5 rows SS starting with P
- 44th row: K1, K2tog, K2, K2tog, K1 (6sts)
- Work 21 rows SS starting with P
- 66th row: K1, inc in next, K2, inc in next, K1 (8sts)
- Work 3 rows SS starting with P
- 70th row: K1, inc in next, K4, inc in next, K1 (10sts)
- Work 3 rows SS starting with P
- 74th row: K1, inc in next, K6, inc in next, K1 (12sts)
- Work 3 rows SS starting with P
- 78th row: K1, K2tog, K6, K2tog, K1 (10sts)
- Work 3 rows SS starting with P
- 82nd row: K1, K2tog, K4, K2tog, K1 (8sts)
- Work 3 rows SS starting with P
- 86th row: K1, K2tog, K2, K2tog, K1 (6sts)
- Work 3 rows SS starting with P
- 90th row: K1, inc in next, K2, inc in next, K1 (8sts)
- 91st row: P
- 92nd row: K1, inc in next, K4, inc in next, K1 (10sts)
- Work 7 rows SS starting with P
- Cast off

To make up: Tie in bow around neck and secure with a few stitches.

NOSE

COLOUR 1

- Size 11/3.00mm needles

- Cast on 8
- 1st row: K
- 2nd row: P2tog, P4, P2tog
- 3rd row: K2tog, K2, K2tog
- 4th row: P4
- 5th row: K2tog, K2tog   (2sts)
- 6th row: K2tog – tie off

To make up: Fold and stitch in place.

HAIR

COLOUR 5

Cut a number of 1-metre lengths of wool. Fold each length over a few times to form small, uncut hanks. Each hank should measure approx. 20cm. Fold each hank and attach to the hairline at the front with fine thread. Place one hank at a time, curl up ends and scrunch into a permanent wave around ears and head. Use small catching stitches to attach to head where necessary.

TO CREATE FACE

Let your inner feelings go on this one! Blue and black yarn or beads for eyes. A red for mouth. The ears are formed from a crocheted chain curled around on itself and stitched together. Add pearl beads for necklace and earrings. The brooch is a sequin shape with added glittery beads.

David and Victoria Beckham

There's famous and then there's ridiculously famous. Posh and Becks are pretty close to the latter now, with stellar careers, vast wealth and fans all over the world. When the talented footballer with Manchester United and England got together with Posh Spice from the Spice Girls it was clear that in partnership they were going to be bigger than they were as individuals. There was a glamorous edge to the young couple that captivated the world of popular culture. Footballer and pop star was a combination to be reckoned with.

David Robert Joseph Beckham was born in Leytonstone, London, in 1975. The Beckhams were an ordinary family, until the talents of young David became clear. Victoria Caroline Adams was born in 1974 in Essex and in 1993 auditioned for a group which would become the Spice Girls. Their first single 'Wannabe' was a global No.1 success and the rest of her singing career is history. When the couple married in 1999, they were already both very famous, but since then there seems to have been no limit to their ambition or popularity. Now a global brand to be reckoned with, Victoria has carved out a new and incredibly successful career in fashion and David's retirement from playing football will give him the opportunity to do pretty much anything he chooses. Posh and Becks, or David and Victoria as they prefer to be known, are a celebrity couple who know how to play the game and are undoubtedly British icons for the modern age.

MATERIALS:
Colour Codes:
1 Rowan Baby Merino Silk DK
(Shade 674 – Shell Pink) – For Body
2 Pure Life Revive Silk
(Shade 00462 – Basalt) – For Suit
3 Regia 4-fädig (4-Ply) Superwash
New Wool (Shade 02905)
– For Shoes
4 John Lewis Own Baby 3-Ply
(White) – For Shirt
5 Rowan Creative Linen
(Shade 628 – Caramel) – For Hair
6 Hank of bronze brown
embroidery yarn – For Tie

Embroidery thread in two tones of
Dark Blonde for Hair
Beads for jacket buttons and eyes
Gold bugle bead for tie pin
Yarn for creating facial features
Stuffing

NEEDLES:
Size 9/3.75mm
Size 10/3.25mm
Size 11/3.00mm
Size 12/2.75mm
Crochet hook 1.50mm
Darning needle

David Beckham

BODY

COLOUR I

- Size 10/3.25mm needles

BODY – FRONT

- Cast on 14
- 1st row: K
- 2nd row: P
- 3rd row: K1 inc in next, K10, inc in next, K1 (16sts)
- Work 5 rows SS starting with P
- 9th row: K1, K2tog, K2, K2tog, K2, K2tog, K2, K2tog, K1 (12sts)
- Work 5 rows SS starting with P
- 15th row: K2, inc in next, K6, inc in next, K2 (14sts)
- 16th row: P
- 17th row: Inc in 1st, K3, inc in next, K4, inc in next, K3, inc in last (18sts)
- 18th row: P
- 19th row: K5, inc in next, K6, inc in next, K5 (20sts)
- 20th row: P
- 21st row: K6, inc in next, K6, inc in next, K6 (22sts)

- 22nd row: P
- 23rd row: K1, sl1, K1, psso, K16, K2tog, K1 (20sts)
- Work 5 rows SS starting with P
- 29th row: K1, sl1, K1, psso, K14, K2tog, K1 (18sts)
- 30th row: P1, P2tog, P12, P2tog, P1 (16sts)
- 31st row: K
- 32nd row: P
- Cast off

BODY – BACK

- Cast on 14
- 1st row: K
- 2nd row: P
- 3rd row: K
- 4th row: P
- 5th row: K2, inc in next, K1, inc in next, K4, inc in next, K1, inc in next, K2 (18sts)
- 6th row: P
- 7th row: K3, inc in next, K1, inc in next, K6, inc in next, K1, inc in next, K3 (22sts)
- Work 3 rows SS starting with P

- 11th row: K1, K2tog, K16, K2tog, K1 (20sts)
- 12th row: P
- 13th row: K2, K2tog, K1, K2tog, K6, K2tog, K1, K2tog, K2 (16sts)
- 14th row: P
- 15th row: K2, K2tog, K2, K2tog, K2tog, K2, K2tog, K2 (12sts)
- Work 5 rows SS starting with P
- 21st row: K1, inc in next, K3, inc in next, inc in next, K3, inc in next, K1 (16sts)
- Work 7 rows SS starting with P
- 29th row: K1, inc in next, K12, inc in next, K1 (18sts)
- 30th row: P
- 31st row: K1, sl1, K1, psso, K12, K2tog, K1 (16sts)
- 32nd row: P1, P2tog, P10, P2tog, P1 (14sts)
- 33rd row: K
- 34th row: P
- Cast off

To make up: Join front and back. Stuff.

HEAD

COLOUR 1
- Size 10/3.25mm needles

RIGHT SIDE OF FACE
- Cast on 5
- 1st row: K
- 2nd row: P
- 3rd row: Cast on 2, K   (7sts)
- 4th row: P5, inc in next, inc in next (9sts)
- 5th row: K1, inc in next, inc in next, K6   (11sts)
- 6th row: P11
- Break thread and leave on needle

LEFT SIDE OF FACE with WS facing
- Cast on 5
- 1st row: K
- 2nd row: P
- 3rd row: K to end, cast on 2   (7sts)
- 4th row: P1, inc in next, inc in next, P4   (9sts)
- 5th row: K6, inc in next, inc in next, K1   (11sts)
- 6th row: P11
- Now join 2 pieces together
- 7th row: K10, K2tog, K10   (21sts)
- 8th row: P1, P2tog, P15, P2tog, P1 (19sts)
- Work 6 rows SS starting with K
- 15th row: K1, sl1, K1, psso, K13, K2tog, K1   (17sts)
- 16th row: P
- 17th row: K1, sl1, K1, psso, K11, K2tog, K1   (15sts)
- 18th row: P
- 19th row: K1, sl1, K1, psso, K9, K2tog K1   (13sts)
- 20th row: P1, P2tog, P7, P2tog, P1 (11sts)
- 21st row: K1, sl1, K1, psso, K5, K2tog, K1   (9sts)
- 22nd row: P
- Cast off

HEAD – BACK
- Cast on 6
- 1st row: K
- 2nd row: P
- 3rd row: K row – inc in 1st and last (8sts)
- 4th row: P
- 5th row: K row – inc in 1st and last (10sts)
- 6th row: P
- 7th row: K row – inc in 1st and last (12sts)
- 8th row: P
- 9th row: K row – inc in 1st and last (14sts)
- Work 7 rows SS starting with P
- 17th row: K1, sl1, K1, psso, K8, K2tog, K1   (12sts)
- 18th row: P
- 19th row: K1, sl1, K1, psso, K6, K2tog, K1   (10sts)
- 20th row: P
- Cast off

To make up: Join front to back. Stuff.

ARMS – MAKE TWO

WORKING FROM SHOULDER TO WRIST
- Cast on 5
- 1st row: K to end
- 2nd row: P to end
- 3rd row: K row – inc in 1st & last (7sts)
- 4th row: P to end
- 5th row: K row – inc in 1st & last (9sts)
- 6th row: P to end
- Work 24 rows

TO CREATE LEFT HAND
- 31st row: K2, put 2 on pin, K5
- 32nd row: P to end bringing 2 sections together   (7sts)
- 33rd row: K
- 34th row: P
- 35th row: K2tog, K2tog, K2tog, K1
- 36th row: P2tog, P2tog
- Pull thread through

TO CREATE RIGHT HAND
- 31st row: K5, put 2 on pin, K2   (7sts)
- 32nd row: P
- 33rd row: K
- 34th row: P
- 35th row: K1, K2tog, K2tog, K2tog
- 36th row: P2tog, P2tog
- Pull thread through

THUMB – SAME FOR BOTH HANDS
- Put 2sts from pin on double-ended needle
- Join thread, K2
- K2tog as i-cord
- Pull thread through

To make up: Join seams. Stuff. Attach to body.

LEGS – MAKE TWO

COLOUR 3
- Size 11/3.00mm needles

- Cast on 24
- 1st row: K
- 2nd row: P
- 3rd row: K10, K2tog, K2tog, K10 (22sts)
- 4th row: P10, P2tog, P10   (21sts)
- 5th row: K5, K2tog, K1, K2tog, K1 K2tog, K1, K2tog, K5   (17sts)
- 6th row: P

- 7th row: K4, cast off 9, K3   (8sts)
- 8th row: P pulling 2 sections of 4sts together
- Work 4 rows SS starting with K
- 13th row: K1, inc in next, K4, inc in next, K1   (10sts)
- 14th row: P
- Break thread and JOIN COLOUR 1
- Work 6 rows SS starting with K
- 21st row: K1, inc in next, K6, inc in next, K1   (12sts)
- Work 7 rows SS starting with P
- 29th row: K1, inc in next, K8, inc in next, K1   (14sts)
- Work 21 rows SS starting with P
- Cast off

TO CREATE HEEL OF BOOT
- Stitch back seam of boot, pick up 8sts along heel edge of boot from right to left – RS facing
- 1st row: Cast on 1, P9   (9sts)
- 2nd row: Cast on 1, K10   (10sts)
- 3rd row: P1, (P2tog)x4, P1
- Cast off

To make up: Sew-up sole of boot and heel. Stuff boot with offcuts of brown wool rather than white wadding, which tends to show through. Sew leg seams. Attach to body.

SHIRT FRONT

COLOUR 4
- Size 12/2.75mm needles

WORKING FROM HEM TO SHOULDER
- Cast on 16
- Work 16 rows SS starting with K
- 17th row: K1, inc in next, K12, inc in next, K1   (18sts)
- Work 3 rows SS starting with P

- 21st row: K1, inc in next, K14, inc in next, K1   (20sts)
- Work 3 rows SS starting with P
- 25th row: K1, inc in next, K16, inc in next, K1   (22sts)
- Work 7 rows SS starting with P
- Cast off

To make up: Attach to body at shoulders and hips.

SHIRT COLLAR
- Cast on 26
- 1st row: K
- 2nd row: P
- 3rd row: K3, K2tog, K3, K2tog, K6, K2tog, K3, K2tog, K3   (22sts)
- Work 3 rows SS starting with P
- Cast off
- Cast off edge is the neck edge

To make up: Fold in half and press. Attach to doll. Stitch at neck front.

*Tip: All pieces of the suit benefit from steam pressing before making up.

TROUSERS

COLOUR 2
- Size 9/3.75mm needles

RIGHT LEG
- Cast on 18
- Work 12 rows SS starting with K
- 13th row: K2tog, K14, K2tog   (16sts)
- Work 24 rows SS starting with P
- 38th row: Inc in 1st, P14, inc in last   (18sts)
- 39th row: K
- 40th row: Cast off 1, P16   (17sts)
- 41st row: Cast off 1   (16sts)
- Break thread
- Hold on pin

LEFT LEG
- Cast on 18
- K as right leg to row 40
- Knitting legs together:
- 41st row: Cast off 1, K to last stitch together – Knit last stitch with first stitch of right leg – K to end of row   (31sts)
- 42nd row: P
- 43rd row: K
- 44th row: P
- 45th row: K6, K2tog, K15, K2tog, K6   (29sts)
- Work 3 rows SS starting with P
- CHANGE TO COLOUR 3, USE DOUBLE
- 49th row: K
- CHANGE TO COLOUR 2
- 50th row: P
- 51st row: K
- Cast off

To make up: Join leg and crotch seams. Add to doll.

JACKET

COLOUR 2
- Size 9/3.75mm needles

FRONT AND BACK – LEFT
- Cast on 20
- Work 10 rows SS starting with K
- 11th row: K9, K2tog, K9   (19sts)
- 12th row: P
- Break thread, set aside on pin

FRONT AND BACK – RIGHT
- Cast on 22
- Work 10 rows SS starting with K
- 11th row: K9, K2tog, K11   (21sts)
- 12th row: Cast off 2, P18   (19sts) turn –

TO JOIN JACKET PIECES TOGETHER

- With RS facing work row 13 across front and back right, followed by front and back left
- 13th row: K18, K next 2sts together, K18   (37sts)
- 14th row: P
- 15th row: K11, K2tog, K11, K2tog, K11   (35sts)
- 16th row: P
- 17th row: K
-

TO START LAPELS

- 18th row: Inc in 1st, P33, inc in last   (37sts)
- 19th row: P1, K11, inc in next, K11, inc in next, K11, P1   (39sts)
- 20th row: K2, P35, K2
- 21st row: P2, K11, inc in next, K11, inc in next, K11, P2   (41sts)
- 22nd row: K3, P35, K3
- 23rd row: P3, K35, P3
- 24th row: K3, P7, inc in next, P19, inc in next, P7, K3 (43sts)
- 25th row: P3, K37, P3

STARTING ARMHOLES

- Working on first 13 stitches front left – put other stitches on pin –
- 26th row: K4, P9
- 27th row: Cast off 1, K7, P4   (12sts)
- 28th row: K4, P6, P2tog   (11sts)
- 29th row: K7, P4
- 30th row: K4, P7
- 31st row: K7, P4
- 32nd row: Cast off 4, P6   (7sts)
- 33rd row: K5, K2tog   (6sts)
- 34th row: P6
- 35th row: K4, K2tog   (5sts)
- 36th row: P3, inc in next, P1   (6sts)
- Cast off

WORKING ON JACKET BACK –

Next 17 stitches – WS facing –

- 26th row: P17
- Work 8 rows SS starting with K
- 35th row: Cast off 4, K12   (13sts)
- 36th row: Cast off 4, P8   (9sts)
- Cast off

WORKING ON FRONT RIGHT ON 13 REMAINING STS

- RS facing
- 26th row: P4, K9
- 27th row: Cast off 1, P7, K4   (12sts)
- 28th row: P4, K6, K2tog   (11sts)
- 29th row: P7, K4   (11sts)
- 30th row: P4, K7
- 31st row: P7, K4
- 32nd row: Cast off 4, K6   (7sts)
- 33rd row: P5, P2tog   (6sts)
- 34th row: K6
- 35th row: P4, K2tog   (5sts)
- 36th row: K3, inc in next, K1   (6sts)
- Cast off

To make up: Join shoulder seams. Catch top of vent.

UPPER COLLAR

Working with WS facing and from right to left, one needle in right hand only, pick up and knit 6sts from front-left neck edge, 8sts from back neck edge, 6sts from front-right neck edge   (20sts)

- 1st row: P
- 2nd row: K7, inc in next, K4, inc in next, K7   (22sts)
- 3rd row: P
- 4th row: K
- Cast off

To make up: Steam press to tidy collar and lapels.

JACKET SLEEVES – MAKE TWO

- Cast on 13
- Work 9 rows SS starting with P
- 10th row: K11, inc in next, K1   (14sts)
- **For second sleeve 10th row to read K1, inc in next, K11**
- Work 11 rows SS starting with P
- 22nd row: Cast off 2, K11   (12sts)
- 23rd row: Cast off 2, P9   (10sts)
- 24th row: K2tog, K6, K2tog   (8sts)
- 25th row: P8
- 26th row: K2tog, K4, K2tog   (6sts)
- 27th row: P2tog, P2, P2tog   (4sts)
- Cast off

To make up: Join seams. Inset to jacket. To finish the suit dress doll and add beads as front and cuff buttons.

TIE

COLOUR 6

- Size 12/2.75mm needles

- Cast on 7
- Work 22 rows SS starting with K
- 23rd row: K3, K2tog, K2   (6sts)
- Work 3 rows SS starting with P
- 27th row: K2, K2tog, K2   (5sts)
- Work 12 rows SS starting with P
- 40th row: K2, K2tog, K1   (4sts)
- Work SS starting with P until work measures 21cm long
- Cast off

To make up: Steam-iron flat, fold wide end into point and stitch into place. Place around neck so that it lies under collar. Wrap narrow end around twice to form knot and secure with stitch. Add gold bugle bead as tie pin.

HAIR

COLOUR 5 – PARE DOWN A SMALL AMOUNT TO 3 STRANDS

- Size 11/3.00mm needles

- Cast on 10
- 1st row: K
- 2nd row: P
- 3rd row: K – inc in 1st & last   (12sts)
- 4th row: P
- 5th row: K – inc in 1st & last   (14sts)
- 6th row: P
- 7th row: K – inc in 1st, K2, inc in next, K2, inc in next, inc in next, K2, inc in next, K2, inc in next   (20sts)
- 8th row: P
- 9th row: K16, turn –
- 10th row: P12, turn –
- 11th row: K16
- 12th row: P16, turn –
- 13th row: K12, turn –
- 14th row: P
- 15th row: K
- 16th row: Cast on 3, P row   (23st)
- 17th row: Cast on 3, K row   (26sts)
- Cast off

To make up: Attach to head to give short back and sides, from crown to nape of neck. To cover the crown, creating the longer top and sides of hair, use lengths of wool and embroidery threads in long broken stitches. Create height at the front and crown by making a small wad with COLOUR 5. Stitch on and cover with more stitches in COLOUR 5, and the two embroidery shades. Vary colours to give natural look. Work in sideburns. Use crochet hook to work in shorter strands at front of hairline. Chop short to stand up.

STUBBLE

To create '5 o'clock shadow', use a pastel pencil and rub gently on upper lip and beard area.

NOSE

COLOUR 1

- Size 12/2.75mm needles
- Cast on 6
- 1st row: K
- 2nd row: P1, P2tog, P1   (4sts)
- 3rd row: K
- 4th row: P1, P2tog, P1   (3sts)
- 5th row: K3
- Pull thread through 3sts

To make up: Attach to face.

Add beads for eyes. Add mouth in yarn of choice.

EARS

- 2 crochet chains stitched on to face

You will need

Note: This figure has wire inserted to legs and body to create pose and stability. For a child-friendly version, omit the wire and create stilettos with i-cord.

MATERIALS:
Colour Codes:
1 Rowan Baby Merino DK (Shade 674 – Shell Pink) – For Body
2 Debbie Bliss Rialto 4-Ply (Shade 22012 – Duck Egg Blue) – For Dress**
3 Debbie Bliss Rialto Lace (Shade 44020 – Hyacinth) – For Bag
4 Debbie Bliss Rialto Lace (Shade 005 – Black) – For Sunglasses
5 Rowan Cotton Glace (Shade 843 – Rich Brown) – For Hair***
6 Debbie Bliss Baby Cashmerino (Shade 340011 – Brown) – For Hair***
7 Debbie Bliss Rialto DK (Shade 012 – Red) – For Shoe Soles (or any Red DK) – small amount required

**We loved the colour of this yarn, but knew that the dress needed to be finer than 4-Ply so we wound off some small balls of yarn halving the ply – this is more easily achieved with a second pair of hands! An alternative would be to use a Rialto Lace 2-Ply in an alternative colour.

***Yarns 5 & 6 are for Victoria's hair. Small quantities are required, and you might prefer to use whatever you have to hand.

Embroidery thread – 2 hanks in different tones of brown for Hair
Small beads for earrings, ring and catch of bag
Small quantity black millinery wire
White millinery wire
Strong beading wire – 24-gauge
Yarn for creating facial features
Masking tape
Jewellery pliers
Wire snips
Stuffing

NEEDLES:
Size 14/2.00mm
Size 13/2.25mm
Size 12/2.75mm
Size 11/3.00mm
Size 11/3.00mm double-ended
Crochet hooks – 1.50mm, 3.00mm & 3.50mm
Darning needle

Victoria Beckham

BODY

COLOUR 1
- Size 11/3.00mm needles

BODY –FRONT
- Cast on 14
- 1st row: K
- 2nd row: P
- 3rd row: K2, inc in next, K8, inc in next, K2   (16sts)
- 4th row: P
- 5th row: K
- 6th row: P1, P2tog, P2, P2tog, P2, P2tog, P2, P2tog, P1   (12sts)
- 7th row: K
- 8th row: P
- 9th row: K2tog, K8, K2tog   (10sts)
- 10th row: P2tog, P6, P2tog   (8sts)
- Work 4 rows SS starting with K
- 15th row: K2, inc in next, K2, inc in next, K2   (10sts)
- 16th row: P
- 17th row: K1, inc in next, K6, inc in next, K1   (12sts)
- 18th row: P
- 19th row: K1, inc in next, K2, inc in next, K2, inc in next, K2, inc in next, K1   (16sts)
- Work 6 rows SS starting with P
- 26th row: P1, P2tog, P10, P2tog, P1 (14sts)
- 27th row: K
- 28th row: P
- 29th row: K1, sl1, K1, psso, K8, K2tog, K1   (12sts)
- 30th row: P
- Cast off

BODY – BACK
- Cast on 16
- 1st row: K
- 2nd row: P
- 3rd row: K3, inc in next, K2, inc in next, K2, inc in next, K2, inc in next, K3   (20sts)
- 4th row: P16, turn –
- 5th row: K12, turn –
- 6th row: P16
- 7th row: K1, K2tog, K3, K2tog, K4, K2tog, K3, K2tog, K1   (16sts)
- 8th row: P1, P2tog, P8, turn –
- 9th row: K6, turn –
- 10th row: P8, P2tog, P1   (14sts)
- 11th row: K1, K2tog, K2, K2tog, K2tog, K2, K2tog, K1   (10sts)
- Work 5 rows SS starting with P
- 17th row: K1, inc in next, K6, inc in next, K1   (12sts)
- 18th row: P
- 19th row: K4, inc in next, K2, inc in next, K4   (14sts)
- Work 5 rows SS starting with P
- 25th row: K1, inc in next, K10, inc in next, K1   (16sts)
- 26th row: P
- 27th row: K1, inc in next, K12, inc in next, K1   (18sts)
- 28th row: P
- 29th row: K1, sl1, K1, psso, K12, K2tog, K1   (16sts)
- 30th row: P
- 31st row: K1, sl1, K1, psso, K10, K2tog, K1   (14sts)
- 32nd row: P
- Cast off

To make up: Join front and back. Stuff.

BUST – MAKE TWO

COLOUR 1
- Size 12/2.75mm needles

- Cast on 18
- 1st row: K
- 2nd row: (P1, P2tog)x6   (12sts)
- 3rd row: K2tog, K1, K2tog, K1, K2tog, K1, K2tog, K1   (8sts)
- 4th row: P2tog, P1, P2tog, P1, P2tog   (5sts)
- Break wool and pull through 5sts, tie off

To make up: Sew-up sides. Place over a bead or marble and steam to shape. Stuff.

ARMS – MAKE TWO

COLOUR 1
- Size 12/2.75mm needles

WORKING FROM SHOULDER TO WRIST
- Cast on 4
- 1st row: K
- 2nd row: P
- 3rd row: K row – inc in 1st & last   (6sts)
- 4th row: P
- 5th row: K row – inc in 1st & last   (8sts)
- Work 13 rows SS starting with P
- 19th row: K2tog, K4, K2tog   (6sts)
- 20th row: P
- 21st row: K2, inc in next, inc in next, K2   (8sts)
- Work 3 rows SS starting with P
- 25th row: K3, K2tog, K3   (7sts)
- 26th row: P
- 27th row: K
- 28th row: P2tog, P3, P2tog   (5sts)
- Work 4 rows SS starting with K
- 33rd row: K row – inc in 1st, K1, inc in next, K1, inc in last   (8sts)

FOR LEFT HAND
- 34th row: P4, inc in next, P3   (9sts)
- 35th row: K2, put 2 on pin, K5
- Work 3 rows SS starting with P
- 39th row: K2tog, K2tog, K2tog, K1   (4sts)
- 40th row: P2tog, P2tog
- Pull wool through

FOR RIGHT HAND
- 34th row: P3, inc in next, P4   (9sts)
- 35th row: K5, put 2 on pin, K2
- Work 3 rows SS starting with P
- 39th row: K1, K2tog, K2tog, K2tog   (4sts)
- 40th row: P2tog, P2tog
- Pull wool through

THUMBS – SAME FOR BOTH HANDS
- Put 2sts from pin on double-ended needle
- Join thread – K2, K2tog as i-cord
- Pull wool through

To make up: Join seams. Stuff. Attach to body.

HEAD

COLOUR 1
- Size 11/3.00mm needles

FRONT-RIGHT OF FACE
- Cast on 3
- Work 4 rows SS starting with K
- 5th row: Cast on 3, K row   (6sts)
- 6th row: P – inc in 1st, P5   (7sts)
- Break wool, hold sts on left-hand needle

FRONT-LEFT OF FACE
- Cast on 3 on same needle
- Now, working on these 3sts only:
- Work 5 rows SS starting with K
- 6th row: Cast on 3, P6, inc in last   (7sts)
- 7th row: K across 2 pieces to join – K6, K2tog, K6   (13sts)
- 8th row: P
- 9th row: K row – inc in 1st & last   (15sts)
- Work 3 rows SS starting with P
- 13th row: K row – inc in 1st & last   (17sts)
- Work 3 rows SS starting with P
- 17th row: K2tog, K13, K2tog   (15sts)
- 18th row: P
- 19th row: K2tog, K11, K2tog   (13sts)
- 20th row: P
- 21st row: K1, sl1, K1, psso, K7, K2tog, K1   (11sts)
- 22nd row: P
- 23rd row: K1, sl1, K1, psso, K5, K2tog, K1   (9sts)
- 24th row: P
- Cast off

HEAD – BACK
- Cast on 3
- 1st row: K
- 2nd row: P
- 3rd row: K
- 4th row: P
- 5th row: K – inc in 1st & last   (5sts)
- 6th row: P
- 7th row: K – inc in 1st & last   (7sts)
- 8th row: P
- 9th row: K – inc in 1st & last   (9sts)
- 10th row: P
- 11th row: K – inc in 1st & last   (11sts)
- 12th row: P
- 13th row: K1, inc in next, K2, inc in next, K1, inc in next, K2, inc in next, K1   (15sts)

- Work 7 rows SS starting with P
- 21st row: K2tog, K3, K2tog, K1, K2tog, k3, K2tog   (11sts)
- 22nd row: P
- 23rd row: K1, sl1, K1, psso, K5, K2tog, K1   (9sts)
- 25th row: P
- Cast off

To make up: Join front to back. Stuff.

LEGS – MAKE TWO
COLOUR 2
- Size 11/3.00mm needles

- Cast on 2
- 1st row: K2
- 2nd row: P row – inc in 1st & 2nd
- 3rd row: K1, inc in next, inc in next, K1   (6sts)
- 4th row: P
- 5th row: K1, inc in next, K2, inc in next, K1   (8sts)
- 6th row: P
- CHANGE TO COLOUR 1
- 7th row: K1, inc in next, K1, inc in next, inc in next, K1, inc in next, K1   (12sts)
- 8th row: P2tog, P8, P2tog   (10sts)
- 9th row: K2tog, K6, K2tog   (8sts)
- Work 3 rows SS starting with P
- 13th row: Cast on 2, K10
- 14th row: Cast on 2, P12
- 15th row: K2tog, K2, K2tog, K2tog, K2, K2tog   (8sts)
- 16th row: P
- 17th row: K2tog, K4, K2tog   (6sts)
- 18th row: P2, P2tog, P2   (5sts)
- Work 6 rows SS starting with K
- 25th row: K1, inc in next, K1, inc in next, K1   (7sts)
- 26th row: P
- 27th row: K
- 28th row: P1, inc in next, P3, inc in

next, P1   (9sts)
- 29th row: K
- 30th row: P
- 31st row: K1, inc in next, K5, inc in next, K1   (11sts)
- Work 6 rows SS starting with P
- 38th row: P1, P2tog, P5, P2tog, P1 (9sts)
- 39th row: K1, sl1, K1, psso, K3, K2tog, K1   (7sts)
- Work 3 rows SS starting with P
- 43rd row: K1, inc in next, K3, inc in next, K1   (9sts)
- Work 4 rows SS starting with P
- 48th row: P1, inc in next, P5, inc in next, P1   (11sts)
- Work 3 rows SS starting with K
- 52nd row: P1, inc in next, P7, inc in next, P1   (13sts)
- Work 5 rows SS starting with K
- 58th row: P1, inc in next, P9, inc in next, P1   (15sts)
- Work 3 rows SS starting with K
- 62nd row: P1, inc in next, P12, inc in next, P1   (17sts)
- 63rd row: K
- Cast off

To make up: Stitch seam under foot to heel. Stuff foot.

TO MAKE STILETTO AND TO WIRE THE LEG
Cut a length of white millinery wire approx. 50cm, fold in half and thread the folded end through the heel of the foot from the inside, leaving approx. 1.5cm of wire protruding to form the stiletto. Secure the heel of the shoe to the foot with a few tight stitches. Sew-up leg seam, stuffing firmly as you go, with very small quantities of wadding at a time – a small pair of pointed scissors works well for this. Leave top of legs open. Join legs together at inner thighs.

TO MAKE UP BODY
Join leg wires together with tape or beading wire, starting approx. 3cm above top of legs to create spine, for approx. 6cm. For the arms, attach a cross-wise piece of beading wire, approx. 25cm long, to the spine with fine wire or tape, checking length of body-to-arms with the knitted body pieces. Join side seams of body, back & front piece. Feed this knitted piece over the wire structure. Stitch body to top of legs all round. Stuff body. Stitch across shoulders, leaving gap for head. Sew-up head front from neck to chin and join front to back leaving a gap for stuffing. Stuff head and close gap. Cut spine to required length to fit within head – turn down the raw end of wire and bind with tape. Attach head to body, pushing spine into head. Place knitted arm pieces over wire arms and cut wire to length – turn over the raw end of wire and bind with tape. Close arm seams, working from the hands to shoulders, shaping and stuffing as you go. Attach at shoulders. Attach bust to front body. Curve spine to gentle S-shape.

HANDBAG
COLOUR 3 – USE YARN DOUBLE
- Size 12/2.75mm needles

- Cast on 10
- Work 4 rows SS starting with K
- 5th row: K row – inc in 1st & last (12sts)
- Work 3 rows SS starting with P
- 9th row: Cast on 3, K15
- 10th row: Cast on 3, P18
- Work 28 rows SS starting with K
- Cast off

To make up: Steam press. Fold in half and

sew side seams of bag to ¾ of the way down from the top. Push in at either side to create gussets – secure with stitch at top. Using wool double, on double-ended needles make a 3-stitch i-cord handle approx. 6cm long. Attach to bag. Add bead fastening to flap.

DRESS

COLOUR 2 (SEE NOTE MATERIALS)
- Size 14/2.00mm needles

DRESS – FRONT
- Size 14/2.00mm needles

- Cast on 22
- 1st row: K
- **Change to 13/2.25mm needles**
- 2nd row: P
- Work 10 rows SS starting with K
- 13th row: K row – inc in 1st & last (24sts)
- Work 11 rows SS starting with P
- 25th row: K row – inc in 1st & last (26sts)
- Work 19 rows SS starting with P
- 45th row: K row – inc in 1st & last (28sts)
- Work 5 rows SS starting with P
- 51st row: K2tog, K24, K2tog   (26sts)
- 52nd row: P
- 53rd row: K2tog, K22, K2tog   (24sts)
- 54th row: P
- 55th row: K2tog, K20, K2tog   (22sts)
- 56th row: P
- 57th row: K7, K2tog, K4, K2tog, K7 (20sts)
- 58th row: P
- 59th row: K2tog, K5, K2tog, K2, K2tog, K5, K2tog   (16sts)
- Work 5 rows SS starting with P
- 65th row: K5, inc in next, K4, inc in next, K5   (18sts)
- 66th row: P

- 67th row: K5, inc in next, K6, inc in next, K5   (20sts)
- 68th row: P
- 69th row: K5, inc in next, K8, inc in next, K5   (22sts)
- 70th row: P
- 71st row: K5, inc in next, K10, inc in next, K5   (24sts)
- 72rd row: P
- 73th row: K5, inc in next, K12, inc in next, K5   (26sts)
- 74th row: P
- 75th row: (K2, inc in next)x8, K2 (34sts)
- Work 3 rows SS starting with P
- 79th row: K2tog, K30, K2tog   (32sts)
- Work 3 rows SS starting with P
- 83rd row: Cast off 2, K5, K2tog, K2, K2tog, K4, K2tog, K2, K2tog, K8 (26sts)
- 84th row: Cast off 2, P23   (24sts)
- 85th row: K9, K2tog, K2, K2tog, K9 (22sts)
- 86th row: P
- 87th row: K3, K2tog, K1, K2tog, K6, K2tog, K1, K2tog, K3   (18sts)
- 88th row: P
- 89th row: K5, K2tog, K4, K2tog, K5 (16sts)
- 90th row: P
- 91st row: K1, inc in next, K12, inc in next, K1   (18sts)
- 92nd row: P
- 93rd row: K
- Cast off

DRESS – BACK LEFT
- **Change to 14/2.00mm needles**
- Cast on 14
- 1st row: K
- **Change to 13/2.25mm needles**
- 2nd row: P
- Work 10 rows SS starting with K
- 13th row: K13, inc in last   (15sts)

- Work 3 rows SS starting with P
- 17th row: K row – cast off 2, break yarn, hold sts on pin

DRESS – BACK RIGHT
- **Change to 14/2.00mm needles**
- Cast on 11
- 1st row: K
- **Change to 13/2.25mm needles**
- 2nd row: P
- Work 10 rows SS starting with K
- 13th row: K – inc in 1st, K10   (12sts)
- Work 3 rows SS starting with P

TO JOIN BACK RIGHT & LEFT
- 17th row: K11, K next with 1st of Back Left, K12   (24sts)
- Work 23 rows SS starting with P
- 41st row: K3, inc in next, K3, inc in next, K2, inc in next, K2, inc in next, K2, inc in next, K3, inc in next, K3 (30sts)
- 42nd row: P
- 43rd row: K23, turn –
- 44th row: P16, turn –
- 45th row: K23
- 46th row: P
- 47th row: K1, K2tog, K3, K2tog, K3, K2tog, K4, K2tog, K3, K2tog, K3, K2tog, K1   (24sts)
- 48th row: P
- 49th row: K1, K2tog, K18, K2tog, K1 (22sts)
- 50th row: P15, turn –
- 51st row: K8, turn
- 52nd row: P15
- 53rd row: K1, K2tog, K16, K2tog, K1 (20sts)
- 54th row: P
- 55th row: K1, K2tog, K14, K2tog, K1 (18sts)
- 56th row: P
- 57th row: K5, K2tog, K4, K2tog, K5 (16sts)

- 58th row: P
- 59th row: K5, K2tog, K2, K2tog, K5 (14sts)
- Work 5 rows SS starting with P
- 65th row: Inc in 1st, K3, inc in next, K4, inc in next, K3, inc in last   (18sts)
- 66th row: P
- 67th row: Inc in 1st, K4, inc in next, K6, inc in next, K4, inc in last   (22sts)
- Work 13 rows SS starting with P

TO CREATE ARMHOLES
- 81st row: K2tog, K18, K2tog   (20sts)
- Work 6 rows SS starting with P
- Cast off

To make up: Steam press both pieces. Catch together the vent at back. Place on doll and join at shoulders. Pin sides to fit exactly. Sew together on the doll – she really is sewn into this dress!

SUNGLASSES (LENSES – MAKE TWO)

*Tip: For a good fit it may be helpful to add ears and nose before adding the glasses. See 'To Create Face'.

COLOUR 4
- Size 14/2.00mm needles
- Cast on 6
- 1st row: P
- 2nd row: K row – inc in 1st & last (8sts)
- 3rd row: P
- 4th row: K row – inc in 1st & last (10sts)
- Work 4 rows SS starting with P
- 9th row: P2tog, P6, P2tog   (8sts)
- 10th row: K
- 11th row: P2tog, P4, P2tog   (6sts)
- 12th row: K
- Cast off

To make up: Press flat. Using jewellery pliers, shape arms and upper-front frame of sunglasses out of black millinery wire, taking measurements from head of doll. Stitch the top of the lenses to the front frame. Add to face. If you are confident with the jewellery pliers, you can shape the bottom frame of the glasses too, joining and doubling the wiring of the arms. Stitch lenses on all round.

HAIR

Using COLOUR 5 and 1.50mm crochet hook, knot in short lengths of yarn to head. Work around the hairline only, gathering onto the top of the head as you go. Trim down and fold over into a knot. Secure at top-back of head with a couple of stitches. This gives a good colour, height and cover to work on. Using COLOUR 6, the two embroidery threads, and working with just a few strands at a time stitch in lengths of yarn onto the crown of the head, where the parting would be. Pay particular attention to the front hairline. Work in a few long strands at the nape. When you feel the hair looks full enough, trim down with hairdressing scissors. To give movement to the look, dampen ends with wet fingers and tweak to shape. Allow to dry.

TO CREATE FACE

For nose, crochet a chain using 3.50mm hook. Fold in half, stitch together and add to face. Repeat for ears.
Using a fine yarn and colour of your choice, add mouth.

TO CREATE RED LOUBOUTIN SOLES FOR SHOES – MAKE TWO

COLOUR 7
- Size 12/2.75mm needles

- Cast on 2
- Work 6 rows SS starting with K
- 7th row: Inc in next, inc in next   (4sts)
- 8th row: P
- 9th row: K
- 10th row: P
- 11th row: K2tog, K2tog   (2sts)
- Cast off

To make up: Stitch sole to shoe.

To complete shoes: Use COLOUR 2 and 3.00mm crochet hook make a length of 5 chain. Put stiletto heel through first loop and catch with stitch. Rest of chain runs up heel of shoe to ankle. Catch in place. Make additional chains as decorative shoe straps, as per photo. Bind stiletto heel with length of COLOUR 2, holding in place with dab of glue.

To complete look, add earrings and ring on left hand.

Ant and Dec

That cheeky Geordie duo Anthony McPartlin and Declan Donnelly have established themselves firmly at the forefront of British television. If you like your entertainment light and with a cheeky sense of humour then Ant and Dec are your guys. With hits starting way back on *Byker Grove*, where they cut their acting teeth, to *SMTV Live*, *Pop Idol*, *Saturday Night Takeaway*, *I'm a Celebrity . . . Get Me Out of Here!*, *Red or Black?* and *Britain's Got Talent*, they've won more National Television Awards than there are snakes in the jungle or humiliated celebrities. Well, nearly. In the 1990s they also had a successful pop career as PJ & Duncan, although they didn't manage a No.1 single until the 2013 re-release of 'Let's Get Ready to Rhumble', with profits going to the charity Childline.

Although they've had their share of controversies over the years, including a bit of a spat with Kelly Brook, Ant and Dec have found a winning formula and stuck with it. They work together, hang out together and even wrote their autobiography together. All of which makes them a formidable team.

The downside of always appearing together was that lots of people couldn't remember which was Ant and which was Dec. The similar suits and Geordie accents really fooled people, despite the fact that they don't look much alike. Fortunately there is a foolproof answer and because they always stand in the same places when they're on the telly, you know it's Ant on the left and Dec on the right – Ant and Dec. Might be trickier if you meet them in the pub, though.

You will need

MATERIALS:
Colour Codes:
1 Rowan Baby Merino Silk DK
(Shade SH674 – Shell Pink) – For Body
2 Debbie Bliss Rialto 4-Ply
(Shade 22003 – Black) – For Tuxedo,
Trousers, Shoes and Hair
3 John Lewis Baby 4-Ply (White) –
For Shirt Front and Collar
4 Debbie Bliss Rialto Lace
(Shade 004 – Charcoal Grey) –
For Tie and to add to Hair

Stuffing
Hank of black embroidery thread
to add to hair
Black beads for jacket buttons
Beads for eyes
Yarn to create face

NEEDLES:
Size 10/3.25mm
Size 12/2.75mm double-ended
Size 14.200mm needles
Crochet hook – 2.00mm and 3.50mm
Darning needle

Anthony McPartlin

BODY

COLOUR 1
- Size 10/3.25mm needles

BODY – FRONT
- Cast on 14
- 1st row: K
- 2nd row: P
- 3rd row: K1, inc in next, K10, inc in next, K1 (16sts)
- Work 3 rows SS starting with P
- 7th row: K1, K2tog, K2, K2tog, K2, K2tog, K2, K2tog, K1 (12sts)
- Work 5 rows SS starting with P
- 13th row: K2, inc in next, K6, inc in next, K2 (14sts)
- 14th row: P
- 15th row: Inc in 1st, K3, inc in next, K4, inc in next, K3, inc in last (18sts)
- 16th row: P
- 17th row: K5, inc in next, K6, inc in next, K5 (20sts)
- Work 3 rows SS starting with P
- 21st row: K1, sl1, K1, psso, K14, K2tog, K1 (18sts)

- Work 5 rows SS starting with P
- 27th row: K1, sl1, K1, psso, K12, K2tog, K1 (16sts)
- 28th row: P1, P2tog, P10, P2tog, P1 (14sts)
- 29th row: K
- 30th row: P
- Cast off

BODY – BACK
- Cast on 14
- 1st row: K
- 2nd row: P
- 3rd row: K2, inc in next, K1, inc in next, K4, inc in next, K1, inc in next, K2 (18sts)
- 4th row: P
- 5th row: K3, inc in next, K1, inc in next, K6, inc in next, K1, inc in next, K3 (22sts)
- Work 3 rows SS starting with P
- 9th row: K1, K2tog, K16, K2tog, K1 (20sts)
- 10th row: P
- 11th row: K2, K2tog, K1, K2tog, K6, K2tog, K1, K2tog, K2 (16sts)
- 12th row: P
- 13th row: K2, K2tog, K2, K2tog, K2tog, K2, K2tog, K2 (12sts)
- Work 4 rows SS starting with P
- 18th row: P3, inc in next, P4, inc in next, P3 (14sts)
- 19th row: K1, inc in next, K4, inc in next, inc in next, K4, inc in next, K1 (18sts)
- Work 9 rows SS starting with P
- 29th row: K1, sl1, K1, psso, K12, K2tog, K1 (16sts).
- 30th row: P1, P2tog, P10, P2tog, P1 (14sts)
- 31st row: K1, sl1, K1, psso, K8, K2tog, K1 (12sts)
- 32nd row: P
- Cast off

To make up: Join front to back. Stuff.

HEAD

COLOUR 1
- Size 10/3.25mm needles

HEAD – FRONT (RIGHT SIDE)

- Cast on 5
- 1st row: K
- 2nd row: P
- 3rd row: Cast on 2, K to end   (7sts)
- 4th row: P5, inc in next, inc in next (9sts)
- 5th row: K1, inc in next, inc in next, K6 (11sts)
- 6th row: P11 – Break wool, leave sts on needle

HEAD – FRONT (LEFT SIDE)

- With WS facing cast on 5, turn – Now working on these 5sts only:
- 1st row: K
- 2nd row: P
- 3rd row: K, cast on 2   (7sts)
- 4th row: P1, inc in next, inc in next, P4 (9sts)
- 5th row: K6, inc in next, inc in next, K1 (11sts)
- 6th row: P11
- 7th row: K across 2 pieces to join, K10, K2tog, K10 (21sts)
- 8th row: P1, P2tog, P15, P2tog, P1 (19sts)
- Work 6 rows SS starting with K
- 15th row: K1, sl1, K1, psso, K13, K2tog, K1 (17sts)
- 16th row: P
- 17th row: K1, sl1, K1, psso, K11, K2tog, K1 (15sts)
- 18th row: P
- 19th row: K1, sl1, K1, psso, K9, K2tog, K1 (13sts)
- 20th row: P1, P2tog, P7, P2tog, P1 (11sts)
- 21st row: K1, sl1, K1, psso, K5, K2tog, K1 (9sts)
- 22nd row: P
- Cast off

HEAD – BACK

- Cast on 4
- 1st row: K
- 2nd row: P
- 3rd row: K
- 4th row: P row – inc in 1st & last (6sts)
- 5th row: K row – inc in 1st & last (8sts)
- 6th row: P
- 7th row: K row – inc in 1st & last (10sts)
- 8th row: P
- 9th row: K row – inc in 1st & last (12sts)
- Work 7 rows SS starting with P
- 17th row: K1, sl1, K1, psso, K8, K2tog, K1   (10sts)
- 18th row: P
- 19th row: K1, sl1, K1, psso, K6, K2tog, K1   (8sts)
- 20th row: P
- Cast off

To make up: Join seam under chin. Join front and back together. Stuff. Attach to body.

ARMS – MAKE TWO

COLOUR 1

- Size 10/3.25mm needles

WORKING FROM SHOULDER TO WRIST

- Cast on 5
- 1st row: K
- 2nd row: P
- 3rd row: K row – inc in 1st & last (7sts)
- 4th row: P
- 5th row: K row – inc in 1st & last (9sts)
- 6th row: P
- Work 24 rows SS starting with K

TO CREATE LEFT HAND

- 31st row: K2, put 2 on pin, K5
- 32nd row: P to end bringing 2 sections together   (7sts)
- 33rd row: K
- 34th row: P
- 35th row: K2tog, K2tog, K2tog, K1
- 36th row: P2tog, P2tog
- Pull thread through

TO CREATE RIGHT HAND

- 31st row: K5, put 2 on pin, K2   (7sts)
- 32nd row: P
- 33rd row: K
- 34th row: P
- 35th row: K1, K2tog, K2tog, K2tog
- 36th row: P2tog, P2tog
- Pull thread through

THUMB – SAME FOR BOTH HANDS

COLOUR 1

- Size 12/2.75mm double-ended needles

- Put 2sts from pin on double-ended needle
- Join thread, K2
- K2tog as i-cord
- Pull thread through

To make up: Join seams. Stuff.

LEGS – MAKE TWO

COLOUR 4

- Size 10/3.25mm needles

- Cast on 24
- 1st row: K
- 2nd row: P
- 3rd row: K10, K2tog, K10   (22sts)
- 4th row: P10. P2tog, P10   (21sts)
- 5th row: K5, (K2tog, K1)x3, K2tog, K5 (17sts)

- 6th row: P
- 7th row: K4, cast off 9, K3   (8sts)
- 8th row: P, pulling 2 sections of 4 together
- Work 4 rows SS starting with K
- 13th row: K1, inc in next, K4, inc in next, K1   (10sts)
- 14th row: P
- CHANGE TO COLOUR 1
- Work 6 rows SS starting with K
- 21st row: K1, inc in next, K6, inc in next, K1   (12sts)
- Work 7 rows SS starting with P
- 29th row: K1, inc in next, K8, inc in next, K1   (14sts)
- Work 18 rows SS starting with P
- Cast off

To make up: Sew-up foot. Stuff with offcuts of black wool rather than white wadding, which tends to show through. Join leg seams. Stuff with wadding. Use black embroidery thread for shoelaces.

SHIRT FRONT

COLOUR 3
- Size 12/2.75mm double-ended needles

- Cast on 20
- Work 34 rows SS starting with P
- 35th row: K10, turn –
- Now working on these 10sts:
- 36th row: Cast off 2, P7   (8sts)
- 37th row: K8
- 38th row: P2tog, P6   (7sts)
- 39th row: K7
- Cast off

- Join wool at centre neck
- 35th row: Cast off 2, K7   (8sts)
- 36th row: P
- 37th row: K2tog, K6   (7sts)
- 38th row: P
- Cast off

To make up: Attach to body at shoulders and hips.

COLLAR
- Cast on 24
- Work 7 rows SS starting with K
- Cast off

To make up: Fold and press. Attach around neck. Catch at centre-front to shirt front.

TIE

COLOUR 4
- Size 14/2.00mm needles

- Cast on 7
- Work 22 rows SS starting with K
- 23rd row: K3, K2tog, K2   (6sts)
- Work 3 rows SS starting with P
- 27th row: K2, K2tog, K2   (5sts)
- Work 12 rows SS starting with P
- 40th row: K2, K2tog, K1   (4sts)
- Work SS starting with P until work measures 21cm long
- Cast off

To make up: Steam-iron flat, fold wide end into point and stitch into place. Place around neck so that it lies under collar. Wrap narrow end around twice to form knot and secure with stitch.

TUXEDO

COLOUR 2
- Size 12/2.75mm double-ended needles

BACK
- Cast on 18
- Work 14 rows SS starting with K
- 15th row: K1, sl1, K1, psso, K12, K2tog, K1   (16sts)

- 16th row: P
- 17th row: K
- Set aside on pin

FRONT RIGHT
- Cast on 19
- 1st row: P
- 2nd row: K
- 3rd row: P
- 4th row: K1, inc in next, K17   (20sts)
- 5th row: P
- 6th row: K1, inc in next, K10, K2tog, K6   (20sts)
- 7th row: P
- 8th row: K1, inc in next, K10, K2tog, K6   (20sts)
- 9th row: P
- 10th row: K1, inc in next, K10, K2tog, K6   (20sts)
- 11th row: P
- 12th row: K1, K2tog, K17   (19sts)
- 13th row P
- 14th row: K8, P5, K6 – to mark top of pocket
- 15th row: P
- 16th row: K
- Set aside on pin

FRONT LEFT
- Cast on 19
- 1st row: P
- 2nd row: K
- 3rd row: P
- 4th row: K17, inc in next, K1   (20sts)
- 5th row: P
- 6th row: K6, sl1, K1, psso, K10, inc in next, K1   (20sts)
- 7th row: P
- 8th row: K6, sl1, K1, psso, K10, inc in next, K1   (20sts)
- 9th row: P
- 10th row: K6, sl1, K1, psso, K10, inc in next, K1   (20sts)
- 11th row: P

- 12th row: K17, K2tog, K1 (19sts)
- 13th row: P
- 14th row: K6, P5, K8 – to mark top of pocket
- 15th row: P
- 16th row: K

To form the two vents in the jacket with the back overlapping the two front pieces: Working onto left-hand needle, with RS facing, slip 17sts of front left, 1st of back, 18th of front left, 2nd of back, 19th of front left, 12sts of back, 1st of front right, 15th of back, 2nd of front right, 16th of back, 17sts of front right (54sts)

- 17th row: P17, P2tog, P2tog, P12, P2tog, P2tog, P17 (50sts)
- 18th row: K
- 19th row: P5, P2tog, P6, P2tog, P7, P2tog, P2, P2tog, P7, P2tog, P6, P2tog, P5 (44sts)
- 20th row: K
- 21st row: P
- 22nd row: K
- 23rd row: P
- 24th row: K
- 25th row: P
- 26th row: K
- 27th row: P
- 28th row: K
- 29th row: P1, inc in next, P4, inc in next, P5, inc in next, P5, P2tog, P4, P2tog, P5, inc in next, P5, inc in next, P4, inc in next, P1 (48sts)
- 30th row: P2, K1, inc in next, K40, inc in next, K1, P2 (50sts)
- 31st row: K3, P44, K3
- 32nd row: P3, K44, P3
- 33rd row: K3, P44, K3
- 34th row: P4, K42, P4
- 35th row: K4, P42, K4
- 36th row: P4, K42, P4

TO CREATE LEFT FRONT

- 37th row: K5, P8, P2tog, turn (14sts)
- 38th row: K9, P5
- 39th row: K5, P9
- 40th row: K9, P5
- 41st row: K6, P8
- 42nd row: K8, P6
- 43rd row: K6, P8
- 44th row: K8, P6
- 45th row: Cast off 3, K2, P8 (11sts)
- 46th row: K6, K2tog, put 3sts on pin – turn (7sts)
- 47th row: P2tog, P5 (6sts)
- 48th row: K6
- 49th row: P6
- 50th row: Cast off 2, K3 (4sts)
- Cast off

TO CREATE BACK – With WS facing join wool

- 37th row: P2tog, P16, P2tog – turn (18sts)
- Work 13 rows SS starting with K
- 51st row: Cast off 5, P7, cast off 5, pull wool through

TO CREATE RIGHT FRONT – With WS facing join wool

- 37th row: P2tog, P8, K5
- 38th row: P5, K9
- 39th row: P9, K5
- 40th row: P5, K9
- 41st row: P8, K6
- 42nd row: P6, K8
- 43rd row: P8, K6
- 44th row: P6, K8
- 45th row: P8, K6
- 46th row: Cast off 3, P2, put these 3 sts onto a pin, K2tog, K6 (7sts)
- 47th row: P5, P2tog (6sts)
- 48th row: K6
- 49th row: Cast off 2, P3 (4sts)
- Cast off

To make up: Join shoulder seams.

TOP COLLAR

- With WS facing
- 1st row: K3sts from left front neck, pick-up 4sts along left front neck, K8sts from back neck, pick-up 4sts along right front neck, K3 from right front neck (22sts)
- 2nd row: P
- 3rd row: K1, inc in next, K4, inc in next, K8, inc in next, K4, inc in next, K1 (26sts)
- 4th row: P
- 5th row: K
- Cast off
- Catch collar at centre back to hold in place

JACKET SLEEVES – MAKE TWO

COLOUR 2

- Size 12/2.75mm double-ended needles

- Cast on 18
- Work 16 rows starting with K
- 17th row: K1, inc in next, K14, inc in next, K1 (20sts)
- Work 14 rows SS starting with P
- 32nd row: Cast off 3, P16 (17sts)
- 33rd row: Cast off 3, K13 (14sts)
- 34th row: P2tog, P10, P2tog (12sts)
- 35th row: K
- 36th row: P2tog, P8, P2tog (10sts)
- 37th row: K2tog, K6, K2tog (8sts)
- Cast off, purling 2 together at each end

- To make up: Sew sleeves seams. Inset into jacket. Catch collar at centre back to hold in place. Add beads for buttons. Using COLOUR 3 work 1 stitch on jacket front left as edge of pocket handkerchief.

TROUSERS

COLOUR 2

- Size 12/2.75mm double-ended needles

TO CREATE FIRST LEG

- Cast on 22
- Work 55 rows SS starting with P
- 56th row: K9, inc in next, K2, inc in next, K9   (24sts)
- 57th row: P
- 58th row: Cast off 2, K to end (22sts)
- 59th row: Cast off 2, P to end   (20sts)
- 60th row: K
- Put on pin

Repeat rows 1 to 60 to create second leg.

KNITTING LEGS TOGETHER

- With WS facing
- 61st row: P19 from second leg, P together last st from second leg and 1st st from first leg, P19 form first leg (39sts)
- Work 8 rows SS starting with K
- 70th row: K8, K2tog, K19, K2tog, K8 (37sts)
- 71st row: P
- 72nd row: K
- 73rd row: P
- Cast off

To make up: Join leg and crotch seams. Attach to doll.

HAIR

COLOUR 2

- Size 10/3.25mm needles

- Cast on 12
- 1st row: K
- 2nd row: P
- 3rd row: K2, inc in next, K6, inc in next, K2   (14sts)
- 4th row: P4, inc in next, P4, inc in next, P4   (16sts)
- 5th row: K1, inc in next, K2, inc in next, K6, inc in next, K2, inc in next, K1   (20sts)
- Work 3 rows SS starting with P
- 9th row: K1, inc in next, K3, K2tog, K6, K2tog, K3, inc in next, K1   (20sts)
- 10th row: Cast on 3, P to end   (23sts)
- 11th row: Cast on 3, K to end   (26sts)
- 12th row: P2, P2tog, P4, P2tog, P6, P2tog, P4, P2tog, P2   (22sts)
- 13th row: K1, K2tog, K16, K2tog, K1 (20sts)
- 14th row: Cast off 2, P17   (18sts)
- 15th row: Cast off 2, K15   (16sts)
- 16th row: P2, P2tog, P2, P2tog, P2tog, P2, P2tog, P2   (12sts)
- 17th row: Cast off 2, K9   (10sts)
- 18th row: Cast off 2, P7   (8sts)
- 19th row: K8
- 20th row: P1, P2tog, P2, P2tog, P1 (6sts)
- 21st row: K1, K2tog, K2tog, K1   (4sts)
- 22nd row: P2tog, P2tog
- Cast off

To make up: Using photo reference, sew hair to head after positioning ears (see To Create Face). Lift hair at centre front by tucking a small piece of wadding under hairline. Using black embroidery thread, add a few long stitches at the sides and back to give a textured look. Using the 2.00mm crotchet hook insert and knot short lengths of COLOUR 4 mixed with a few strands of the black embroidery thread over the crown area. Trim.

TO CREATE FACE

- The nose and ears are crocheted chains in flesh colour, stitched to head and face. Use own choice of wool for eyes, brows and mouth.

You will need

MATERIALS:
Colour Codes:
1 Rowan Baby Merino Silk DK
(Shade SH674 – Shell Pink) – For Body
2 Debbie Bliss Rialto 4-Ply
(Shade 22003 – Black) – For Tuxedo,
Trousers and Shoes
3 John Lewis Baby 4-Ply (White) –
For Shirt Front and Collar
4 Debbie Bliss Rialto Lace
(Shade 004 – Charcoal Grey) –
For Tie
5 Regia 4-Fadig (4-Ply)
Superwashed New Wool
(Shade 02905 – Brown) – For Hair

Stuffing
Two shades of brown embroidery
thread to add into hair
Hank of light brown embroidery
thread to add into hair
Black beads for jacket buttons
Beads for eyes
Yarn to create face

NEEDLES:
Size 10/3.25mm
Size 12/2.75mm double-ended
Size 14/2.00mm
Crochet hook – 3.50mm
Darning needle

Declan Donnelly

BODY

COLOUR 1
- Size 10/3.25mm needles

BODY – FRONT
- Cast on 14
- 1st row: K
- 2nd row: P
- 3rd row: K1, inc in next, K10, inc in next, K1   (16sts)
- Work 2 rows SS starting with P
- 6th row: P1, P2tog, P2, P2tog, P2, P2tog, P2, P2tog, P1   (12sts)
- Work 4 rows SS starting with K
- 11th row: K2, inc in next, K6, inc in next, K2   (14sts)
- 12th row: P
- 13th row: Inc in 1st, K3, inc in next, K4, inc in next, K3, inc in last   (18sts)
- 14th row: P
- 15th row: K5, inc in next, K6, inc in next, K5   (20sts)
- Work 2 rows SS starting with P
- 18th row: P1, P2tog, P14, P2tog, P1   (18sts)

- Work 4 rows SS starting with K
- 23rd row: K1, sl1, K1, psso, K12, K2tog, K1   (16sts)
- 24th row: P1, P2tog, P10, P2tog, P1 (14sts)
- 25th row: K
- 26th row: P
- Cast off

BODY – BACK
- Cast on 14
- 1st row: K
- 2nd row: P
- 3rd row: K2, inc in next, K1, inc in next, K4, inc in next, K1, inc in next, K2   (18sts)
- 4th row: P
- 5th row: K3, inc in next, K1, inc in next, K6, inc in next, K1, inc in next, K3   (22sts)
- Work 2 rows SS starting with P
- 8th row: P1, P2tog, P16, P2tog, P1 (20sts)
- 9th row: K
- 10th row: P2, P2tog, P1, P2tog, P6,

P2tog, P1, P2tog, P2   (16sts)
- 11th row: K2, K2tog, K2, K2tog, K2tog, K2, K2tog, K2   (12sts)
- Work 3 rows SS starting with P
- 15th row: K3, inc in next, K4, inc in next, K3   (14sts)
- 16th row: P1, inc in next, P4, inc in next, inc in next, P4, inc in next, P1 (18sts)
- Work 8 rows SS starting with K
- 25th row: K1, sl1, K1, psso, K12, K2tog, K1   (16sts).
- 26th row: P1, P2tog, P10, P2tog, P1 (14sts)
- 27th row: K1, sl1, K1, psso, K8, K2tog, K1   (12sts)
- 28th row: P
- Cast off

To make up: Join front to back. Stuff.

HEAD

COLOUR 1
- Size 10/3.25mm needles

HEAD – FRONT (RIGHT SIDE)
- Cast on 5
- 1st row: K
- 2nd row: P
- 3rd row: Cast on 2, K to end   (7sts)
- 4th row: P4, inc in next, inc in next , P1   (9sts)
- 5th row: K1, inc in next, K1, inc in next, K5   (11sts)
- 6th row: P11 – Break wool, leave sts on needle

HEAD – FRONT (LEFT SIDE)
- With WS facing cast on 5, turn – Now working on these 5sts only:
- 1st row: K
- 2nd row: P
- 3rd row: K, cast on 2   (7sts)
- 4th row: P1, inc in next, inc in next, P4   (9sts)
- 5th row: K5, inc in next, K1, inc in next, K1   (11sts)
- 6th row: P11
- 7th row: K across 2 pieces to join, K7, inc in next, K2, K2tog, K2, inc in next, K7   (23sts)
- 8th row: P1, P2tog, P17, P2tog, P1   (21sts)
- Work 6 rows SS starting with K
- 15th row: K1, sl1, K1, psso, K15, K2tog, K1   (19sts)
- 16th row: P
- 17th row: K1, sl1, K1, psso, K13, K2tog, K1   (17sts)
- 18th row: P4, P2tog, P5, P2tog, P4   (15sts)
- 19th row: K1, sl1, K1, psso, K9, K2tog, K1   (13sts)
- 20th row: P1, P2tog, P7, P2tog, P1   (11sts)
- 21st row: K1, sl1, K1, psso, K5, K2tog, K1   (9sts)
- Cast off

HEAD – BACK
- Cast on 4
- 1st row: K
- 2nd row: P
- 3rd row: K
- 4th row: P row – inc in 1st & last (6sts)
- 5th row: K row – inc in 1st & last (8sts)
- 6th row: P
- 7th row: K row – inc in 1st & last (10sts)
- Work 10 rows SS starting with P
- 18th row: P1, P2tog, P6, P2tog, P1 (8sts)
- 19th row: K
- Cast off

To make up: Join seam under chin. Join front and back together. Stuff. Attach to body.

ARMS – MAKE TWO
COLOUR 1
- Size 10/3.25mm needles

WORKING FROM SHOULDER TO WRIST
- Cast on 5
- 1st row: K
- 2nd row: P
- 3rd row: K row – inc in 1st & last (7sts)
- 4th row: P
- 5th row: K row – inc in 1st & last (9sts)
- 6th row: P
- Work 22 rows SS starting with K

TO CREATE LEFT HAND
- 31st row: K2, put 2 on pin, K5
- 32nd row: P to end bringing 2 sections together   (7sts)
- 33rd row: K

- 34th row: P
- 35th row: K2tog, K2tog, K2tog, K1
- 36th row: P2tog, P2tog
- Pull thread through

TO CREATE RIGHT HAND
- 31st row: K5, put 2 on pin, K2   (7sts)
- 32nd row: P
- 33rd row: K
- 34th row: P
- 35th row: K1, K2tog, K2tog, K2tog
- 36th row: P2tog, P2tog
- Pull thread through

THUMB – SAME FOR BOTH HANDS
COLOUR 1
- Size 12/2.75mm double-ended needles

- Put 2sts from pin on double-ended needle
- Join thread, K2
- K2tog as i-cord
- Pull thread through

To make up: Join seams. Stuff

LEGS – MAKE TWO
COLOUR 4
- Size 10/3.25mm needles

- Cast on 24
- 1st row: K
- 2nd row: P
- 3rd row: K10, K2tog, K10   (22sts)
- 4th row: P10. P2tog, P10   (21sts)
- 5th row: K5, (K2tog, K1)x3, K2tog, K5 (17sts)
- 6th row: P
- 7th row: K4, cast off 9, K3   (8sts)
- 8th row: P, pulling 2 sections of 4 together
- Work 4 rows SS starting with K

- 13th row: K1, inc in next, K4, inc in next, K1   (10sts)
- 14th row: P
- CHANGE TO COLOUR 1
- Work 6 rows SS starting with K
- 21st row: K1, inc in next, K6, inc in next, K1   (12sts)
- Work 5 rows SS starting with P
- 27th row: K1, inc in next, K8, inc in next, K1   (14sts)
- Work 15 rows SS starting with P
- Cast off

To make up: Sew-up foot. Stuff with offcuts of black wool rather than white wadding, which tends to show through. Join leg seams. Stuff with wadding. Use black embroidery thread for shoelaces.

SHIRT FRONT

COLOUR 3

- Size 12/2.75mm needles

- Cast on 20
- Work 34 rows SS starting with P
- 35th row: K10, turn –
- Now working on these 10sts:
- 36th row: Cast off 2, P7   (8sts)
- 37th row: K8
- 38th row: P2tog, P6   (7sts)
- 39th row: K7
- Cast off

- Join wool at centre neck
- 35th row: Cast off 2, K7   (8sts)
- 36th row: P
- 37th row: K2tog, K6   (7sts)
- 38th row: P
- Cast off

To make up: Attach to body at shoulders and hips.

COLLAR

- Cast on 24
- Work 7 rows SS starting with K
- Cast off

To make up: Fold and press. Attach around neck. Catch at centre-front to shirt front.

TIE

COLOUR 4

- Size 14/2.00mm needles

- Cast on 7
- Work 22 rows SS starting with K
- 23rd row: K3, K2tog, K2   (6sts)
- Work 3 rows SS starting with P
- 27th row: K2, K2tog, K2   (5sts)
- Work 12 rows SS starting with P
- 40th row: K2, K2tog, K1   (4sts)
- Work SS starting with P until work measures 21cm long
- Cast off

To make up: Steam-iron flat, fold wide end into point and stitch into place. Place around neck so that it lies under collar. Wrap narrow end around twice to form knot and secure with stitch.

TUXEDO

COLOUR 2

- Size 12/2.75mm double-ended needles

BACK

- Cast on 18
- Work 14 rows SS starting with K
- 15th row: K1, sl1, K1, psso, K12, K2tog, K1   (16sts)
- 16th row: P
- 17th row: K
- Set aside on pin

FRONT RIGHT

- Cast on 19
- 1st row: P
- 2nd row: K
- 3rd row: P
- 4th row: K1, inc in next, K17   (20sts)
- 5th row: P
- 6th row: K1, inc in next, K10, K2tog, K6   (20sts)
- 7th row: P
- 8th row: K1, inc in next, K10, K2tog, K6   (20sts)
- 9th row: P
- 10th row: K1, inc in next, K10, K2tog, K6   (20sts)
- 11th row: P
- 12th row: K1, K2tog, K17   (19sts)
- 13th row P
- 14th row: K8, P5, K6 – to mark top of pocket
- 15th row: P
- 16th row: K
- Set aside on pin

FRONT LEFT

- Cast on 19
- 1st row: P
- 2nd row: K
- 3rd row: P
- 4th row: K17, inc in next, K1   (20sts)
- 5th row: P
- 6th row: K6, sl1, K1, psso, K10, inc in next, K1   (20sts)
- 7th row: P
- 8th row: K6, sl1, K1, psso, K10, inc in next, K1   (20sts)
- 9th row: P
- 10th row: K6, sl1, K1, psso, K10, inc in next, K1   (20sts)
- 11th row: P
- 12th row: K17, K2tog, K1   (19sts)
- 13th row: P
- 14th row: K6, P5, K8 – to mark top of pocket

- 15th row: P
- 16th row: K

To form the two vents in the jacket with the back overlapping the two front pieces: Working onto left-hand needle, with RS facing, slip 17sts of front left, 1st of back, 18th of front left, 2nd of back, 19th of front left, 12sts of back, 1st of front right, 15th of back, 2nd of front right, 16th of back, 17sts of front right (54sts)

- 17th row: P17, P2tog, P2tog, P12, P2tog, P2tog, P17 (50sts)
- 18th row: K
- 19th row: P5, P2tog, P6, P2tog, P7, P2tog, P2, P2tog, P7, P2tog, P6, P2tog, P5 (44sts)
- 20th row: K
- 21st row: P
- 22nd row: K
- 23rd row: P
- 24th row: K
- 25th row: P1, inc in next, P4, inc in next, P5, inc in next, P5, P2tog, P4, P2tog, P5, inc in next, P5, inc in next, P4, inc in next, P1 (48sts)
- 26th row: P2, K1, inc in next, K40, inc in next, K1, P2 (50sts)
- 27th row: K3, P44, K3
- 28th row: P3, K44, P3
- 29th row: K3, P44, K3
- 30th row: P4, K42, P4
- 31st row: K4, P42, K4
- 32nd row: P4, K42, P4

TO CREATE LEFT FRONT
- 33rd row: K5, P8, P2tog, turn (14sts)
- 34th row: K9, P5
- 35th row: K5, P9
- 36th row: K9, P5
- 37th row: K6, P8
- 38th row: K8, P6

- 39th row: K6, P8
- 40th row: K8, P6
- 41st row: Cast off 3, K2, P8 (11sts)
- 42nd row: K6, K2tog, put 3sts on pin – turn (7sts)
- 43rd row: P2tog, P5 (6sts)
- 44th row: K6
- 45th row: P6
- 46th row: Cast off 2, K3 (4sts)
- Cast off

TO CREATE BACK –
With WS facing join wool
- 33rd row: P2tog, P16, P2tog – turn (18sts)
- Work 13 rows SS starting with K
- 47th row: cast off 5, P7, cast off 5, pull wool through

TO CREATE RIGHT FRONT –
With WS facing join wool
- 33rd row: P2tog, P8, K5
- 34th row: P5, K9
- 35th row: P9, K5
- 36th row: P5, K9
- 37th row: P8, K6
- 38th row: P6, K8
- 39th row: P8, K6
- 40th row: P6, K8
- 41st row: P8, K6
- 42nd row: Cast off 3, P2, put these 3 sts onto a pin, K2tog, K6 (7sts)
- 43rd row: P5, P2tog (6sts)
- 44th row: K6
- 45th row: Cast off 2, P3 (4sts)
- Cast off

To make up: Join shoulder seams.

TOP COLLAR
- With WS facing
- 1st row: K3sts from left front neck, pick up 4sts along left front neck, K8 sts from back neck, pick-up 4sts along

right front neck, K3 from right front neck (22sts)
- 2nd row: P
- 3rd row: K1, inc in next, K4, inc in next, K8, inc in next, K4, inc in next, K1 (26sts)
- 4th row: P
- 5th row: K
- Cast off
- Catch collar at centre back to hold in place

JACKET SLEEVES – MAKE TWO
COLOUR 2
- Size 12/2.75mm needles

- Cast on 18
- Work 16 rows starting with K
- 17th row: K1, inc in next, K14, inc in next, K1 (20sts)
- Work 12 rows SS starting with P
- 30th row: Cast off 3, P16 (17sts)
- 31st row: Cast off 3, K13 (14sts)
- 32nd row: P2tog, P10, P2tog (12sts)
- 33rd row: K
- 34th row: P2tog, P8, P2tog (10sts)
- 35th row: K2tog, K6, K2tog (8sts)
- Cast off, purling 2 together at each end

To make up: Sew seams. Inset into jacket. Catch collar at centre back to hold in place. Add beads for jacket buttons. Using COLOUR 3 work stitch on left jacket front for edge of pocket handkerchief.

TROUSERS
COLOUR 2
- Size 12/2.75mm needles

TO CREATE FIRST LEG

- Cast on 22
- Work 47 rows SS starting with P
- 48th row: K9, inc in next, K2, inc in next, K9   (24sts)
- 49th row: P
- 50th row: Cast off 2, K to end (22sts)
- 51st row: Cast off 2, P to end   (20sts)
- 52nd row: K
- Put on pin

Repeat rows 1 to 52 to create second leg.

KNITTING LEGS TOGETHER
- With WS facing
- 53rd row: P19 from second leg, P together last st from second leg and 1st st from first leg, P19 form first leg (39sts)
- Work 8 rows SS starting with K
- 62nd row: K8, K2tog, K19, K2tog, K8 (37sts)
- 63rd row: P
- 64th row: K
- 65th row: P
- Cast off

To make up: Join leg and crotch seams. Attach to doll.

HAIR
COLOUR 5
- Size 10/3.25mm needles

- Cast on 12
- 1st row: K
- 2nd row: P
- 3rd row: K2, inc in next, K6, inc in next, K2   (14sts)
- 4th row: P4, inc in next, P4, inc in next, P4   (16sts)
- 5th row: K1, inc in next, K2, inc in next, K6, inc in next, K2, inc in next, K1   (20sts)

- Work 3 rows SS starting with P
- 9th row: K1, inc in next, K3, K2tog, K6, K2tog, K3, inc in next, K1   (20sts)
- 10th row: Cast on 3, P to end   (23sts)
- 11th row: Cast on 3, K to end   (26sts)
- 12th row: P2, P2tog, P4, P2tog, P6, P2tog, P4, P2tog, P2   (22sts)
- 13th row: K1, K2tog, K16, K2tog, K1 (20sts)
- 14th row: Cast off 2, P17   (18sts)
- 15th row: Cast off 2, K15   (16sts)
- 16th row: P2, P2tog, P2, P2tog, P2tog, P2, P2tog, P2   (12sts)
- 17th row: Cast off 2, K9   (10sts)
- 18th row: Cast off 2, P7   (8sts)
- 19th row: K8
- 20th row: P1, P2tog, P2, P2tog, P1 (6sts)
- 21st row: K1, K2tog, K2tog, K1   (4sts)
- 22nd row: P2tog, P2tog
- Cast off

To make up: Using photo reference, sew hair to head after positioning ears (see To Create Face). Add height to Dec's crown by folding a length of COLOUR 5 yarn over on itself a few times. Stitch to crown. Work over this with broken stitches in the two shades of brown embroidery threads and continue working more stitches into the sides and back. Hook and knot in short lengths across front hairline. Chop short.

TO CREATE FACE
The nose and ears are crocheted chains in flesh colour, stitched to head and face. Use own choice of wool for eyes, brows and mouth.

You will need

MATERIALS:
Colour Codes:
1 Rowan Baby Merino Silk DK
(Shade SH674 – Shell Pink) – For Body
2 Rowan Pure DK (Shade 002 –
Shale) – For Socks
3 Debbie Bliss Baby Cashmerino
(Shade 340008 – Navy) – For Suit
4 MillaMia Sweden Naturally Soft
Merino (Petal 122) – For Shirt
5 Rowan Baby Merino Silk DK
(Shade SH671 – Straw) – For Hair
6 Debbie Bliss Baby Cashmerino
(Black) – For Shoes
7 Hank of blue embroidery yarn
– For Tie

Small buttons for jacket
Yarn for creating facial features
3 to 4 small beads for buttons
of shirt front
Stuffing

NEEDLES:
Size 10/3.25mm
Size 10/3.25mm double-ended
Size 11/3.00mm
Size 12/2.75mm
Crochet hook – 2.00mm & 4.00mm
Darning needle

Boris Johnson

Alexander Boris de Pfeffel Johnson is one of the most colourful politicians we've had for some time. As a constituency politician, he followed the charismatic Michael Heseltine as Member of Parliament for Henley. Both have been known for their unique hairstyles so perhaps it's something they look for in that part of the world.

Despite his boyish looks and somewhat eccentric demeanour, Boris is now a seasoned heavyweight politician who is more than capable of looking after himself. Being Mayor of London, now in his second term in office, he is also, some say, well positioned for high office in the Conservative Party in due course. A future Prime Minister? We shall see.

Boris's career to date has certainly had its ups and downs. One of the high points must surely be his role in London's hugely successful 2012 Olympic Games. It was also one of the few occasions that his unruly hair has been under control. On the downside, Boris has had to weather numerous controversies, from alleged affairs to upsetting the people of Liverpool to calling his rather healthy income from journalism 'chicken feed'. But his ability to survive difficult moments – like getting stuck on a zip wire descent and having to be rescued – with good humour and a thick skin, suggests that we'll be seeing plenty more of Boris Johnson in the future. That's why he's made it into our collection, that and the fun you can have with his hair!

BODY

COLOUR 1

- Size 10/3.25mm needles

BODY – FRONT

- Cast on 16
- 1st row: P
- 2nd row: K1, inc in next, K12, inc in next, K1 (18sts)
- Work 3 rows SS starting with P
- 6th row: K1, inc in next, K14, inc in next, K1 (20sts)
- Work 3 rows SS starting with P
- 10th row: K1, K2tog, K2, K2tog, K6, K2tog, K2, K2tog, K1 (16sts)
- Work 3 rows SS starting with P
- 14th row: K2, inc in next, K2, inc in next, K4, inc in next, K2, inc in next, K2 (20sts)
- 15th row: P
- 16th row: K2, inc in next, K3, inc in next, K6, inc in next, K3, inc in next, K2 (24sts)
- Work 9 rows SS starting with P
- 26th row: K1, sl1, K1, psso, K18, K2tog, K1 (22sts)
- 27th row: P1, P2tog, P16, P2tog, P1 (20sts)
- 28th row: K1, sl1, K1, psso, K14, K2tog, K1 (18sts)
- 29th row: P
- Cast off

BODY – BACK

COLOUR 1

- Size 10/3.25mm needles

- Cast on 16
- 1st row: P
- 2nd row: K2, inc in next, K3, inc in next, K2, inc in next, K3, inc in next, K2 (20sts)
- 3rd row: P

- 4th row: K2, inc in next K14, inc in next, K2 (22sts)
- 5th row: P
- 6th row: K2, inc in next, K16, inc in next, K2 (24sts)
- 7th row: P
- 8th row: K2, inc in next, K18, inc in next, K2 (26sts)
- Work 3 rows SS starting with P
- 12th row: K1, K2tog, K5, K2tog, K6, K2tog, K5, K2tog, K1 (22sts)
- 13th row: P
- 14th row: K2, K2tog, K1, K2tog, K2, K2tog, K2tog, K2, K2tog, K1, K2tog, K2 (16sts)
- Work 5 rows SS starting with P
- 20th row: K2, inc in next, K2, inc in next, K4, inc in next, K2, inc in next, K2 (20sts)
- 21st row: P
- 22nd row: K2, inc in next, K4, inc in next, K4, inc in next, K4, inc in next, K2 (24sts)
- Work 8 rows SS starting with P
- 31st row: P1, P2tog, P18, P2tog, P1 (22sts)
- 32nd row: K1, sl1, K1, psso, K16, K2tog, K1 (20sts)
- Cast off

To make up: Join front and back. Stuff.

ARMS – MAKE TWO

COLOUR 1

- Size 10/3.25mm needles

WORKING FROM SHOULDER TO WRIST

- Cast on 5
- 1st row: K
- 2nd row: P
- 3rd row: K row – inc in 1st & last (7sts)
- 4th row: P

- 5th row: K row – inc in 1st & last (9sts)
- 6th row: P
- Work 26 rows SS starting with K

TO CREATE LEFT HAND

- 33rd row: K2, put 2 on pin, K5
- 34th row: P to end pulling two sections together (7sts)
- 35th row: K
- 36th row: P
- 37th row: K2tog, K2tog, K2tog, K1
- 38th row: P2tog, P2tog, pull wool through

TO CREATE RIGHT HAND

- 33rd row: K5, put 2 on pin, K2 (7sts)
- 34th row: P
- 35th row: K
- 36th row: P
- 37th row: K1, K2tog, K2tog, K2tog
- 38th row: P2tog, P2tog, pull wool through

THUMB – SAME FOR BOTH HANDS

- Put 2sts from pin on double-ended needle, join thread, K2
- K2tog as i-cord
- Pull wool through

To make up: Join seams. Stuff.

LEGS – MAKE TWO

COLOUR 2

- Size 10/3.25mm needles

- Cast on 20
- 1st row: P
- 2nd row: K
- 3rd row: P
- 4th row: K6, K2tog, K1, K2tog, K1, K2tog, K6 (17sts)

- 5th row: P
- 6th row: K4, cast off 9, K3 (8sts)
- 7th row: P, pulling 2 sections of 4sts together
- Work 4 rows SS starting with K
- 12th row: K1, inc in next, K4, inc in next, K1 (10sts)
- 13th row: P
- Break thread
- CHANGE TO COLOUR 1
- Work 6 rows SS starting with K
- 20th row: K1, inc in next, K6, inc in next, K1 (12sts)
- Work 7 rows SS starting with P
- 28th row: K1, inc in next, K8, inc in next, K1 (14sts)
- Work 7 rows SS starting with P
- 36th row: K1, inc in next, K10, inc in next, K1 (16sts)
- Work 7 rows SS starting with P
- Cast off

To make up: Join seams. Stuff.

HEAD

COLOUR 1
- Size10/3.25mm needles

HEAD – FRONT

- Cast on 6
- 1st row: K
- 2nd row: P2, inc in next, inc in next, P2 (8sts)
- 3rd row: K row – inc in 1st & last (10sts)
- 4th row: P
- 5th row: K row – inc in 1st & last (12sts)
- 6th row: P
- 7th row: K row – inc in 1st & last (14sts)
- Work 9 rows SS starting with P
- 17th row: K1, sl1, K1, psso, K8, K2tog, K1 (12sts)
- 18th row: P
- 19th row: K1, sl1, K1, psso, K6, K2tog, K1 (10sts)
- 20th row: P
- Cast off

HEAD – BACK

- Cast on 6
- 1st row: K
- 2nd row: P
- 3rd row: K row – inc in 1st & last (8sts)
- 4th row: P
- 5th row: K row – inc in 1st & last (10sts)
- 6th row: P
- 7th row: Inc in 1st, K2, inc in next, K2, inc in next, K2, inc in last (14sts)
- 8th row: P
- 9th row: Inc in 1st, K2, inc in next, K1, inc in next, K2, inc in next, K1, inc in next, K2, inc in last (20sts)
- Work 3 rows SS starting with P
- 13th row: K5, inc in next, K2, inc in next, K2, inc in next, K2, inc in next, K5 (24sts)
- Work 3 rows SS starting with P
- 17th row: K1, sl1, K1, psso, K3, K2tog, K2tog, K4, K2tog, K2tog, K3, K2tog, K1 (18sts)
- 18th row: P
- 19th row: K1, sl1, K1, psso, (K2tog)x7, K1 (10sts)
- 20th row: P
- Cast off

To make up: Join 2 pieces together. Stuff.

SHIRT FRONT

COLOUR 4 – Pare down wool to 3 strands
- Size 11/3.00mm needles

- Cast on 22
- Work 16 rows SS starting with K
- 17th row: K1, inc in next, K18, inc in next, K1 (24sts)
- Work 11 rows SS starting with P
- 29th row: K1, inc in next, K20, inc in next, K1 (26sts)
- Work 5 rows SS starting with P
- 35th row: K11, K2tog, turn – Now working on these 12sts only
- 36th row: P1, P2tog, P4, turn –
- 37th row: K3, K2tog, K1, turn –
- Cast off

Thread remaining 13sts onto right-hand needle, with WS facing. Join thread at outside edge.

- 35th row: P11, P2tog (12sts)
- 36th row: K1, K2tog, K4, turn –
- 37th row: P3, P2tog, K1, turn –
- Cast off

To make up: Stitch onto body front at shoulders and hips. Add 3 to 4 small white beads as buttons.

COLLAR

COLOUR 4 – pare down to 3 strands
- Size 11/3.00mm needles

- Cast on 28
- Work 5 rows SS starting with K
- Cast off

To make up: Fold in half and press with damp cloth. Attach around neck and to shirt front.

TROUSERS

COLOUR 3
- Size 10/3.25mm needles

TO CREATE FIRST LEG
- Cast on 22
- Work 6 rows SS starting with K
- 7th row: K1, K2tog, K16, K2tog, K1 (20sts)
- 8th row: P
- 9th row: K1, K2tog, K14, K2tog, K1 (18sts)
- 10th row: P
- 11th row: K6, K2tog, K2, K2tog, K6 (16sts)
- Work 3 rows SS starting with P
- 15th row: K6, inc in next, K2, inc in next, K6 (18sts)
- Work 3 rows SS starting with P
- 19th row: K1, inc in next, K14, inc in next, K1 (20sts)
- 20th row: P
- 21st row: K1, inc in next, K16, inc in next, K1 (22sts)
- 22nd row: P
- 23rd row: K8, inc in next, K4, inc in next, K8 (24sts)
- 24th row: P
- 25th row: (K4, inc in next)x4, K4 (28sts)
- Work 5 rows SS starting with P
- 31st row: (K4, K2tog)x4, K4 (24sts)
- Work 9 rows SS starting with P
- 41st row: Cast off 2, K to end
- 42nd row: Cast off 2, P to end (20sts)
- Put on pin

TO CREATE SECOND LEG
- Cast on 22
- Work rows 1 to 42

TO KNIT LEGS TOGETHER
- Starting on left leg:

- 43rd row: K6, K2tog, K4, K2tog, K5, K next st together with 1st st of right leg, K5, K2tog, K4, K2tog, K6 (35sts)
- Work 9 rows SS starting with P
- CHANGE TO COLOUR 6 FOR BELT
- 44th row: K
- 45th row: P
- CHANGE TO COLOUR 3
- 46th row: K
- Cast off

JACKET

COLOUR 3
- Size 10/3.25mm needles

BACK
- Cast on 18
- 1st row: K
- 2nd row: K1, P to last, K1
- Repeat rows 1 & 2 (x5)
- 13th row: K1, K2tog, K12, K2tog, K1 (16sts)
- 14th row: K1, P to last, K1
- 15th row: K
- 16th row: P
- Put on pin

LEFT FRONT
- Cast on 20
- 1st row: K
- 2nd row: K1, P to last, K1
- Repeat rows 1 & 2 (x5)
- 13th row: K5, K2tog, K13 (19sts)
- 14th row: K1, P17, K1
- 15th row: K13, K2tog, K4 (18sts)
- 16th row: K1, P17
- 17th row: Cast off 2
- Put on pin

RIGHT FRONT
- Cast on 20
- 1st row: K
- 2nd row: K1, P to last, K1 (20sts)
- Repeat rows 1 & 2 (x5)

- 13th row: K13, K2tog, K5 (19sts)
- 14th row: K1, P17, K1
- 15th row: K13, K2tog, K4 (18sts)
- 16th row: Cast off 2, P14, K1 (16sts)

TO JOIN JACKET PIECES TOGETHER
- With RS facing put left front, back, right front pieces onto left-hand needle
- 17th row: K15, K2tog, K14, K2tog, K15 (46sts)
- 18th row: K1, P44, K1
- 19th row: K
- 20th row: K1, P44, K1
- 21st row: K
- 22nd row: K1, P12, inc in next, P18, inc in next, P12, K1 (48sts)
- 23rd row: K1, inc in next, K44, inc in next, K1 (50sts)

START OF LAPEL
- 24throw: K2, P46, K2
- 25th row: K1, P1, K46, P1, K1
- 26th row: K3, P44, K3
- 27th row: K1, P2, K44, P2, K1
- 28th row: K1, K3, P11, turn – start of armhole

WORKING NOW ON LEFT FRONT – (15sts) hold remaining sts on pin
- 29th row: K11, P3, K1
- 30th row: K5, P10
- 31st row: K10, P4, K1
- 32nd row: K6, P9
- 33rd row: K9, P5, K1
- 34th row: K7, P8
- 35th row: K8, P6, K1
- 36th row: K8, P7
- 37th row: K7, P7, K1
- 38th row: Cast off 5, K2, P7 (10sts)
- 39th row: K7, P2tog, K1 (9sts)
- 40th row: K2tog, P7 (8sts)
- 41st row: K5, K2tog, P1 (7sts)
- 42nd row: P7
- 43rd row: K5, turn –

- 44th row: P5
- Cast off

WORKING NOW ON RIGHT FRONT – RS FACING – 15STS
Keep remaining sts on pin for back of jacket
- 28th row: KI, P3, KII
- 29th row: PII, K4
- 30th row: KI, P4, KI0
- 31st row: PI0, K5
- 32nd row: KI, P5, K9
- 33rd row: P9, K6
- 34th row: KI, P6, K8
- 35th row: P8, K7
- 36th row: KI, P7, K7
- 37th row: P7, K8
- 38th row: Cast off 5, P2, K7   (10sts)
- 39th row: P7, K2tog, KI   (9sts)
- 40th row: P2tog, K7   (8sts)
- 41st row: P5, P2tog, KI   (7sts)
- 42nd row: K7
- 43rd row: P5, turn –
- 44th row: K5
- Cast off

TO CREATE BACK – RS FACING – 20STS
- 28th row: K
- 29th row: P
- 30th row: KI, inc in next, KI6, inc in next, KI   (22sts)
- Work 9 rows SS starting with P
- 40th row: Cast off 4, KI7   (18sts)
- 41st row: Cast off 4, PI3   (14sts)
- 42nd row: Cast off 3, KI0   (11sts)
- 43rd row: Cast off 3, P7   (8sts)
- Put on pin

To make upper part of suit collar sew shoulder seams of back & front together. Using a smaller-sized needle for ease with WS facing, pick-up 9sts from left front collar edge, 8sts from back, 9sts from

right front collar edge – turn work to RS facing

Revert to 10/3.25mm needles
1st row: P   (26sts)
2nd row: KI, inc in next, K5, inc in next, K3, inc in next, K2, inc in next, K3, inc in next, K5, inc in next, KI   (32sts)
3rd row: P
4th row: KI3, inc in next, K4, inc in next, KI3   (34sts)
Cast off

JACKET SLEEVES – MAKE TWO
COLOUR 4
- Size 10/3.25mm needles

- Cast on 16
- 1st row: P
- CHANGE TO COLOUR 3
- Work 14 rows SS starting with K
- 16th row: KI, inc in next, KI2, inc in next, KI   (18sts)
- Work 9 rows SS starting with P
- 26th row: Cast off 3, KI4   (15sts)
- 27th row: Cast off 3, PII   (12sts)
- 28th row: K2tog, cast off 3, K7   (8sts)
- 29th row: P2tog, cast off 3, P3   (4sts)
- Cast off

To make up: Join seams. Inset in jacket.

SHOES
COLOUR 6
- Size 10/3.25mm needles

- Cast on 22
- 1st row: K
- 2nd row: PI9, turn –
- 3rd row: KI2, turn –
- 4th row: P7, turn –
- 5th row: KII, turn –
- 6th row: PI9

- 7th row: K9, K2tog, K2tog, K9   (20sts)
- 8th row: P8, P2tog, P2tog, P8   (18sts)
- 9th row: K2tog, K2, K2tog, KI, K2tog, K2tog, KI, K2tog, K2, K2tog   (12sts)
- Cast off

To make up: Stitch back centre seam. Stitch underside of shoe. Wet, blot, shape.

TIE
COLOUR 7
- Size 12/2.75mm needles

- Cast on 7
- Work 22 rows SS starting with K
- 23rd row: K3, K2tog, K2   (6sts)
- Work 3 rows SS starting with P
- 27th row: K2, K2tog, K2   (5sts)
- Work 12 rows SS starting with P
- 40th row: K2, K2tog, KI   (4sts)
- Work SS starting with P until work measures 22cm long
- Cast off

To make up: Steam iron flat. Fold wide end into a point and stitch into place. Decide length of tie and where knot should be. Wind narrow end around twice to form knot shape. Stitch in place.

HAIR
Boris's most noted feature is his hair, so it is worth spending some time on this. Using COLOUR 5 cut workable lengths (approx. 40cm) and separate into strands. Press and steam iron with vigour. Knot 3 or 4 strands at a time into the head using the smaller crochet hook. Cut each fixed piece to length before starting on the next piece. Work directionally, bearing in mind no two lengths are the same on Boris's head.

You will need

MATERIALS:
Colour Codes:

1 Debbie Bliss Rialto Lace (Shade 44002 – Pale Grey) – For Windows (use double with Colour 2) & For Radiator Grill
2 Debbie Bliss Rialto Lace (Shade 44012 – Cream) – For Windows (use double with Colour 1)
3 Debbie Bliss Baby Cashmerino (Shade 340070 – Blue)
4 Sublime Extra Fine Merino DK (Shade 0167 – Red)
5 Debbie Bliss Baby Cashmerino (Shade 340101 – White)
6 Lincatex Gold Rush Decorative Thread (Shade 6 – Silver) – For Chrome Trim
7 Patons 100% Cotton DK (Shade 2712 – Black) – For Wheels & Chassis
8 Debbie Bliss Baby Cashmerino (Shade 340300 – Black) – For Stripes on Bonnet
9 Sublime Baby Cashmerino silk DK (Shade 0219 – Orange/Brown) – For Rear Lights
10 Rowan Fine Tweed (Shade 366 – Grey) – For End of Exhaust
11 Rowan Fine Tweed (Shade 373 – Rust) – For Exhaust

BUTTONS
For headlights (2 per car)
Fog lamps (3 per car)
Rear lights (4 per car)
Wheels (4 per car)

Spray glue

2 blocks of foam:
11.50cm x 6.50cm x 2.75cm (for base)
6.00cm x 6.50cm x 2.75cm (for top)
Sheet wadding
Stuffing
Fabric stiffener
All-purpose glue
Black felt for number plates
Pentel Hybrid 1mm gel pen in white for writing number plates

NEEDLES:
Size 12/2.75mm
Size 12/2.75mm double-ended set of 5
Crochet hook 13/2.25mm
Darning needle

Mini

The quintessentially British Mini first arrived on our streets in 1959 and was an instant hit. After the austerity of the post-war years, Britain was just about to emerge into the Swinging Sixties and the arrival of the Mini was perfectly timed. The inspired design by Alec Issigonis with its front-wheel drive layout and transverse engine allowed maximum passenger space in a very small car, and people loved it for its low costs and modern looks. During its lifetime, more than 1.5 million Minis were sold in Britain.

Over the years, there have been many special editions of the Mini but perhaps the most famous is the Mini Cooper. When John Cooper, founder of the Cooper Car Company, suggested the idea of

a sportier version, the Mini Cooper was born and it was so good that it not only became a favourite with buyers but also went on to win the prestigious Monte Carlo Rally in 1964, 1965 and 1967. It also won in 1966 but was disqualified by the French judges on a rather spurious technicality. Perhaps even more famously, Mini Cooper S's starred in the 1969 movie *The Italian Job* as they helped Michael Caine's character Charlie Croker escape with a consignment of stolen gold in Turin by squeezing down alleyways and through sewage pipes to escape.

Although now owned by BMW with new designs and bigger and more modern cars, the original Mini remains an icon that will forever be British.

TO FORM FOAM SHAPE OF MINI

Stick top block to base block with spray glue, positioning top block 1.50cm in from one end of the base block to form the boot. With scissors taper sides of top block to give softer curve up to roof.

WINDOWS

The same for each colour Mini
COLOURS 1 & 2 knitted as double thread
Size 12/2.75mm double-ended set of 5

Cast on 104 on 4 needles as below

Row	Needle 1 – Front	Needle 2 – Side	Needle 3 – Back	Needle 4 – Side	(sts)
Cast on	20	30	20	30	100
1	K	K	K	K	
2	K	K	K	K	
3	K	P2tog, K26, P2tog	K	P2tog, K26, P2tog	96
4	P2tog, K16, P2tog	K	P2tog, K16, P2tog	K	92
5	K	P2tog, K24, P2tog	K	P2tog, K24, P2tog	88
6	K	K	K	K	
7	K	P2tog, K22, P2tog	K	P2tog, K22, P2tog	84
8	P2tog, K14, P2tog	K	P2tog, K14, P2tog	K	80
9	K	P2tog, K20, P2tog	K	P2tog, K20, P2tog	76
10	K	K	K	K	
11	P2tog, K12, P2tog	P2tog, K18, P2tog	P2tog, K12, P2tog	P2tog, K18, P2tog	68
12	K	K	K	K	
13	K	P2tog, K16, P2tog	K	P2tog, K16, P2tog	64
14	K	K	K	K	

Cast off

ROOF

COLOUR 3,4 OR 5

- Size 12/2.75mm needles
- Cast on 12
- 1st row: K
- 2nd row: K
- 3rd row: P
- 4th row: K – inc in next 2, K8, inc in last 2 (16sts)
- 5th row: K1, P to last, K1
- 6th row: K
- Repeat rows 5 and 6 (x9)
- 25th row: P2tog, P2tog, P8, P2tog, P2tog (12sts)
- 26th row: K
- 27th row: K
- Cast off

TO MAKE THE WINDOW FRAMES

- With RS facing pick up 4st around the back left-hand corner and work 14 rows SS, starting with P. Put these onto a pin and leave a length of wool. The exact size of these will be determined when you start assembling the car. Repeat on the back right-hand corner. Do the same at the other end of the roof, picking up 3st on each corner. The edge of the doorframe on each side is a 2st i-cord approx. halfway along the long side to match with the position of the door on the side panel.

SIDE PANELS

COLOUR 3, 4 OR 5

- Size 12/2.75mm needles

RIGHT PANEL

- Cast on 43
- 1st row: K
- 2nd row: K
- 3rd row: K1, P30, K1, P10, K1

- 4th row: K11, P1, K31
- 5th row: K1, P13, K10, P6, K1, P2, turn –
- 6th row: K2, P1, K5, P1, K10, P1, K13
- 7th row: K1, P12, K1, P10, K1, P4, K1, P12, K1
- 8th row: K13, P1, K4, P1, K10, P1, K13
- 9th row: K1, P12, K1, P10, K1, P3, K1, P13, K1
- 10th row: K14, P1, K3, P1, K10, P1, K10, K2tog, K1 (42sts)
- 11th row: K1, P11, K1, P10, K1, P2, K1, P14, K1
- 12th row: K1, (K2tog)x3, K8, P1, K2, P1, K10, P1, K12 (39sts)
- 13th row: K1, P11, K1, P10, K1, P1, K1, P12, K1
- 14th row: Cast off 3, K9, P1, K1, P1, K3, K2tog, K2, K2tog, P1, K2, K2tog, K3, K2tog, K1, K2tog, K1 (31sts)
- 15th row: K1, P9, K1, P7, K2, P7, turn –
- 16th row: K7, P2, K6, P1, K8, K2tog, K1
- 17th row: cast off 20, P9
- 18th row: K7, turn –
- 19th row: P7
- 20th row: K7, K2tog, K1
- 21st row: K1, P2tog, P6
- 22nd row: K6, turn –
- 23rd row: P6
- 24th row: K8
- Cast off

LEFT PANEL

- Cast on 43
- 1st row: K
- 2nd row: K
- 3rd row: K1, P10, K1, P30, K1
- 4th row: K31, P1, K1, turn –
- 5th row: P2, K1, P6, K10, P13, K1
- 6th row: K13, P1, K10, P1, K5, P1, K12
- 7th row: K1, P12, K1, P4, K1, P10, K1, P12, K1
- 8th row: K13, P1, K10, P1, K4, P1, K13
- 9th row: K1, P13, K1, P3, K1, P10, K1,

P12, K1
- 10th row: K1, K2tog, K10, P1, K10, P1, K3, P1, K14 (42sts)
- 11th row: K1, P14, K1, P2, K1, P10, K1, P11, K1
- 12th row: K12, P1, K10, P1, K2, P1, K8, (K2tog)x3, K1 (39sts)
- 13th row: Cast off 3, P9, K1, P1, K1, P10, K1, P11, K1 (36sts)
- 14th row: K1, K2tog, K1, K2tog, K3, K2tog, K2, P1, K2tog, K2, K2tog, K3, P1, K1, P1, K6, turn –
- 15th row: P7, K2, P7, K1, P9, K1
- 16th row: K1, K2tog, K8, P1, K6, P2, K11 (30sts)
- 17th row: P7, turn –
- 18th row: K7
- 19th row: P7, P2tog, K1, turn
- 20th row: K9
- 21st row: P6, turn –
- 22nd row: K6
- 23rd row: P6, P2tog, K1, turn
- 24th row: K8
- Cast off

BOOT

COLOUR 3, 4 OR 5

- Size 12/2.75mm needles
- Cast on 14
- 1st row: K
- 2nd row: K
- 3rd row: K1, P to last, K1
- 4th row: K
- 5th row: K1, inc in next, P3, inc in next, P2, inc in next, P3, inc in next, K1 (18sts)
- 6th row: K6, P6, K6
- 7th row: K1, P4, K1, P6, K1, P4, K1
- 8th row: K4, P1, K8, P1, K4
- 9th row: K1, P2, K1, P10, K1, P2, K1
- 10th row: K3, P1, K10, P1, K3
- 11th row: K1, P2, K1, P10, K1, P2, K1
- 12th row: K3, P1, K10, P1, K3
- 13th row: K1, P3, K1, P8, K1, P3, K1

- 14th row: K5, P8, K5
- 15th row: K1, P to last, K1
- 16th row: K1, K2tog, K3, K2tog, K2, K2tog, K3, K2tog, K1 (14sts)
- 17th row: K1, P to last, K1
- 18th row: K
- Cast off

BONNET

COLOUR 3, 4 OR 5
- Size 12/2.75mm needles
- Cast on 12
- Work 2 rows K
- Work 4 rows SS starting with P
- 7th row: P2, P2tog, P4, P2tog, P2 (10sts)
- Work 4 rows SS starting with K
- 12th row: K4, K2tog, K4 (9sts)
- Work 11 rows SS starting with P
- 24th row: K
- 25th row: K
- Cast off

CHASSIS

COLOUR 8
- Size 12/2.75mm needles
- Cast on 14
- 1st row: K
- 2nd row: K
- 3rd row: P
- 4th row: inc in 1st, inc in next, K10, inc in next, inc in next (18sts)
- Work 5 rows SS starting with P – each P row to have K1 at each end
- Work 3 rows SS starting with P – each P row to have K1 at each end
- Work 30 rows SS starting with P – each P row to have K1 at each end
- 43rd row: K8, P2, K8
- 44th row: K1, P6, K4, P6, K1
- 45th row: K6, P6, K6
- 46th row: K1, P4, K2, inc in next, K2, inc in next, K2, P4, K1

- 47th row: P6, inc in next, P2, inc in next, inc in next, P2, inc in next, P6
- 48th row: K
- 49th row: P6, P2tog, P2, P2tog, P2tog, P2, P2tog, P6
- 50th row: K1, P4, K2, K2tog, K2, K2tog, K2, P4, K1
- 51st row: K6, P6, K6
- 52nd row: K1, P6, K4, P6, K1
- 53rd row: K8, P2, K8
- 54th row: K1, P to last, K1
- 55th row: K2tog, K2tog, K10, K2tog, K2tog (14sts)
- 56th row: K
- 57th row: K
- Cast off

EXHAUST

COLOUR 11
- Size 12/2.75mm double-ended

- With RS facing pick-up 3sts just to the rear of the front axle rib in the centre of the car
- Work as i-cord for 1cm, turn –
- Next row: K1, inc in next, K1, turn – (4sts)
- Work 6 rows SS starting k
- Next row: K1, K2tog, K1 (3sts)
- Work i-cord for 6cm, turn –
- Next row: inc in all sts, turn – (6sts)
- Work 8 rows SS starting k
- Next row: (K2tog)×3 (3sts)
- CHANGE TO COLOUR 10
- Next row: P
- Next row: K
- Next row: Inc in all sts (6sts)
- Work 5 rows SS starting with K
- Cast off

WHEELS – MAKE FOUR

COLOUR 7
- Size 12/2.75mm needles

- Cast on 24
- 1st row: K
- 2nd row: P2tog to end (12sts)
- 3rd row: K
- 4th row: P
- 5th row: K2tog to end (6sts)
- 6th row: P2tog to end (3sts)
- Pull wool through and sew into a disc. Stiffen with fabric stiffener and set aside to dry. Attach silver buttons to centre.

BLACK STRIPES ON BONNET

COLOUR 8
- Crochet hook 2.25mm
- Work approx. 15 chain – confirm length across the bonnet and finish off to fit.

CHROME TRIM

COLOUR 6
- Size 12/2.75mm double-ended
- Work 2 lengths of 2st i-cord approx. 30cm long for the sides
- Work 2 lengths of 3st i-cord approx. 10cm long for the back and front
- Work 4 lengths of 2st i-cord approx. 5cm long for the back and front bumpers

To make up: Lightly press all pieces. Stretch the window piece onto the top block and put a little wadding front and back to make a triangular profile. Stretch the roof section across the top with the 4sts window frame strips at the back, the 3sts strips at the front. Join boot, bonnet and side sections together and pull over the foam block. The back window frame strips should match up to the boot seam and front strip to the corner of the front wing. Pick-up 2sts in the centre of the side roof piece on both sides, work as i-cord to meet the door shape of the side panel. Stitch in place.

The size of the window frame sections should now be clear; tuck inside the door panels and stitch in place. Sew the side sections of the roof to the top of the windows and around the bottom of the windows to the body sections. Put small pieces of sheet wadding around the sides, bonnet, boot and wings. Note that the boot should be proud of the foam base by approx. 1.5cm, so gently shape with wadding to create this profile.

Stitch chassis around the bottom edge, putting a small ball of wadding in the centre of the back axle. Stitch the exhaust across the bottom, curving as necessary to the back left-hand corner. With COLOUR 1, used double, embroider lines for the radiator grill. Pin the wheels in place to match up with the axle detail on the chassis. Stab through the foam base to secure well. Pin and

stitch the 2sts silver trim along the sides to make wheel arches, stopping at the corners. Take the 3sts silver trim pieces, fold the ends in by approx. 1.5cm and make the correct length to fit as back and front bumpers. Fold in the ends of the 2sts short lengths and stitch on as the upright supports for the bumper – two at the front, two at the back. Stitch the completed bumpers in place. Stitch the black chain lengths across the bonnet from the front window to the tip of the radiator grill.

Add buttons for headlamps. Add 3 buttons for fog lamps across the top edge of the radiator. Add buttons for the rear lights on the boot and wind a thread of COLOUR 9 to surround them, and stitch in place. Stiffen two small pieces of black felt, write car registration on them and glue in place front and back.

You will need

MATERIALS:
Colour Codes:
1 Debbie Bliss Baby Cashmerino
(Shade 340011 – Brown) – For Jar
2 Sublime Cashmerino Silk DK
(Shade 0250 – Yellow) – For Lid
3 Rowan Fine Lace
(Shade 00935 – Red) – For Label
4 Rowan Baby Merino Silk DK (Shade
683 – Grass Green) – For Label
5 Patons Fairytale Dreamtime Pure
Wool 2-Ply (Shade 00051 – White) –
For Label

Dark green embroidery thread
for graphics of label
Orange/brown embroidery
thread for label
Sheet of clear acetate,
approx. 25cm x 15cm
Stuffing

NEEDLES:
Size 14/2.00mm
Size 12/2.75mm
Size 12/2.75mm double-ended
Darning needle

Marmite

Love it or hate it, we think Marmite is a British classic. First produced in Burton upon Trent in 1902, the name comes from a type of French cooking pot, which still appears on the label today. Marmite itself is derived from brewer's yeast, which is then processed to become the tangy spread that goes so well on toast, or with cheese.

Marmite is also an excellent source of B-vitamins, some of which are already present, some added during manufacture. During the two World Wars, Marmite was included in soldiers' rations and it's also said to be an excellent defence against mosquitos.

And although it will forever divide opinion between lovers and haters of the rich, dark spread, we think Marmite is an important part of British life and should be treasured and enjoyed. Even if you prefer to knit it rather than eat it.

BASE

COLOUR 1

- Size 12/2.75mm double-ended needles

- Cast on 8
- Put on set of 4 needles, joining into circle
- 1st row: K
- 2nd row: K – inc in every st   (16sts)
- Work 3 rows K
- 6th row: K – inc in every st   (32sts)
- Work 2 rows K
- Cast off very loosely

The reverse side is to be the right side of this piece.

LID

COLOUR 2

- Size 12/2.75mm double-ended needles

- Cast on 48
- Put on set of 4 needles, joining into circle
- Work 5 rows of 1&1 rib
- 6th row: P
- 7th row: K
- 8th row: K
- 9th row: (K1, K2tog) to end   (32sts)
- Work 3 rows K
- 13th row: K2tog to end   (16sts)
- 14th row: K
- 15th row: K2tog to end   (8sts)
- 16th row: K
- Pull wool through

LABEL PANELS

BACK AND FRONT – MAKE TWO COLOUR 2 – PARED DOWN TO 4-PLY

- Size 12/2.75mm needles

- Cast on 14
- 1st row: K
- 2nd row: P row – inc in 1st & last (16sts)
- 3rd row: K row – inc in 1st & last (18sts)
- 4th row: P row – inc in 1st & last (20sts)
- 5th row: K
- 6th row: P row – inc in 1st & last (22sts)
- Work 7 rows SS starting with K
- 14th row: P2tog at beginning & end of row   (20sts)
- 15th row: K
- 16th row: P2tog at beginning & end of row   (18sts)
- 17th row: K2tog at beginning & end of row   (16sts)
- 18th row: P2tog at beginning & end of row   (14sts)
- 19th row: K2tog at beginning & end of row   (12sts)
- Cast off

SIDE PANELS – MAKE TWO

COLOUR 1

- Size 12/2.75mm needles

WORKING FROM COLLAR TO BASE OF JAR

- Cast on 16
- 1st row: K1, P to last, K1
- 2nd row: K1, sl1, K1, psso, K1, (inc in next)x3, K2, (inc in next)x3, K1, K2tog, K1   (20sts)
- 3rd row: K1, P to last, K1
- 4th row: K1, sl1, K1, psso, K5, inc in next, K2, inc in next, K5, K2tog, K1 (20sts)
- 5th row: K1, P to last, K1
- 6th row: K1, (sl1, K1, psso)x2, K10, (K2tog)x2, K1   (16sts)
- 7th row: K1, P to last, K1
- 8th row: K1, sl1, K1, psso, K10, K2tog, K1   (14sts)
- 9th row: K1, P to last, K1
- 10th row: K1, sl1, K1, psso, K3, (inc in next)x2, K3, K2tog, K1   (14sts)
- 11th row: K1, P10, turn –
- 12th row: K8, turn –
- 13th row: P10, K1
- 14th row: K14
- 15th row: K1, P to last, K1
- 16th row: K5, inc in next, K2, inc in next, K5   (16sts)
- 17th row: K1, P to last, K1
- 18th row: K
- 19th row: K1, P4, P2tog, P2, P2tog, P4, K1   (14sts)
- 20th row: K11, turn –
- 21st row: P8, turn –
- 22nd row: K11
- 23rd row: K1, P to last, K1
- 24th row: K1, inc in next, K10, inc in next, K1   (16sts)
- 25th row: K1, P to last, K1
- 26th row: K1, inc in next, K12, inc in next, K1   (18sts)
- 27th row: K1, P to last, K1
- 28th row: K1, inc in next, K14, inc in next, K1   (20sts)
- 29th row: K1, P6, P2tog, P2, P2tog, P6, K1   (18sts)
- 30th row: K1, inc in next, K14, inc in next, K1   (20sts)
- 31st row: K1, P6, P2tog, P2, P2tog, P6, K1   (18sts)
- 32nd row: K1, inc in next, K5, cast off 4, K4, inc in next, K1   (16sts in 2 sets of 8sts)

WORKING ON 8STS:

- 33rd row: K1, P4, P2tog, K1   (7sts)
- 34th row: K1, (sl1, K1, psso)x2, inc in next, K1   (6sts)
- 35th row: K1, P1, (P2tog)x2   (4sts)
- Cast off. Pull wool through

WORKING ON REMAINING 8STS, WS-FACING:

- 33rd row: K1, P2tog, P4, K1   (7sts)
- 34th row: K1, inc in next, (K2tog)x2, K1   (6sts)
- 35th row: (P2tog)x2, P1, K1   (4sts)
- 36th row: K
- Cast off. Pull wool through

To make up: Join cast-off points of side panels at centre-base, creating hole for base of jar. Inset base and sew in place. Note: The wrong side is the outside of the base. Catch corners of cast-on edges together at centre top, creating hole for label panels back & front. Now work collar.

COLLAR

COLOUR 1

- Size 12/2.75mm double-ended needles

- Pick-up 15sts from each cast-on edge of side panels   (30sts)
- Work 12 rounds K
- 11th row: P
- Work 12 rounds K
- Cast off loosely

To make up: Fold down inside neck along P row. Catch in place at base of collar.

LABEL DECORATION

RED RIBBON BANNER
COLOUR 3

- Size 14/2.00mm needles

- Cast on 5
- Work 8 rows SS starting with K
- 9th row: K1, inc in next, K3   (6sts)
- Work 5 rows SS starting with P
- 15th row: K1, inc in next, K4   (7sts)
- Work 12 rows SS starting with P
- 28th row: P1, P2tog, P4   (6sts)
- Work 5 rows SS starting with K
- 34th row: P1, P2tog, P3   (5sts)
- Work 5 rows SS starting with K
- Cast off

WHITE AREA
COLOUR 5

- Size 14/2.00mm needles

- Cast on 16
- 1st row: P
- 2nd row: K2tog, K12, K2tog   (14sts)
- 3rd row: P
- 4th row: K2tog, K10, K2tog   (12sts)
- 5th row: P
- 6th row: K2tog, K8, K2tog   (10sts)
- 7th row: P2tog, P6, P2tog   (8sts)
- 8th row: K2tog, K4, K2tog   (6sts)
- 9th row: P2tog, P2, P2tog   (4sts)
- Cast off

GREEN CURVE
COLOUR 4

- Size 14/2.00mm needles

- Cast on 3sts
- Work approx.16 rows SS starting with K, until the green strip fits nicely under the red banner

To make up: Pin and stitch these 3 pieces onto yellow label panels. Outline banner & green curve in the dark green embroidery thread, write 'Marmite' in white wool on the red banner and create a small jar in the centre of the white area using the orange/brown embroidery thread. Create blocks of colour as writing on rear label – use a real jar of Marmite for reference.

Inset panels to back & front of jar. Cut two pieces of acetate to the shape of the label panels. Insert acetate pieces into jar, holding in place against the label panels with stuffing. Stuff firmly. Cut acetate circle to fit within the lid. To firm-up rim of lid, cut a strip approx. 25cm x 1cm, roll it around on itself and place inside the rim. Add lid to jar & stitch in place.

You will need

MATERIALS:**
Colour Codes:
1   Rowan Wool Cotton 4-Ply
(Shade 00481 – Cream)

24 gauge beads
Jewellery pliers
Wire snips
Stuffing
Sheet wadding
Pastel sticks & fixative, or paint for
colouring

NEEDLES:**
Size 10/3.25mm double-ended
Darning needle

**Note: You will use this material
for both pasty patterns**

Cornish Pasty

The Cornish Pasty is one of the most iconic of British foods. With its rich buttery pastry and meat and vegetable filling, it's a really delicious treat. There are a number of different versions available but the classic beef filling with diced potato and swede is hard to beat. This now has European protection as a Cornish product.

For the Cornish miners, particularly when tin mining was at its height, the pasty was an essential part of their diet as it provided everything they needed in a handy little package and was both tasty and satisfying, sustaining them through a long shift in often difficult and cramped conditions. Nowadays, it's just a great thing to have for your lunch.

There has been some controversy about whether the pasty should be crimped around the edge, like a 'D', or over the top. The protected status pasty is the D-shape but in Cornwall there are many who still advocate the top crimp. It may seem like an academic debate to outsiders but to those who know their pasties, this remains a serious issue. We've gone for both types, so hopefully that'll keep everyone happy!

UPRIGHT PASTY

- Work on 4 needles, joined in a circle
- Cast on 8
- 1st row: K
- 2nd row: Inc in every sts   (16sts)
- 3rd row: K
- 4th row: (K1, inc in next)x8   (24sts)
- 5th row: K
- 6th row: (K2, inc in next)x8   (32sts)
- Work 2 rows K
- 9th row: (K3, inc in next)x8   (40sts)
- Work 2 rows K
- 12th row: (K4, inc in next)x8   (48sts)
- 13th row: K
- 14th row: (K5, inc in next)x8   (56sts)
- Work 2 rows K
- 17th row: (K6, inc in next)x8   (64sts)
- 18th row: K
- 19th row: (K7, inc in next)x8   (72sts)
- Work 2 rows K
- 22nd row: (K8, inc in next)x8   (80sts)
- 23rd row: K
- 24th row: (K9, inc in next)x8   (88sts)
- Work 2 rows K
- 27th row: (K10, inc in next)x8   (96sts)
- 28th row: K
- 29th row: (K11, inc in next)x8 (104sts)
- Work 2 rows K
- 32nd row: (K12, inc in next)x8 (112sts)
- 33rd row: K
- 34th row: (K13, inc in next)x8 (120sts)
- Work 2 rows K
- 37th row: (K14, inc in next)x8 (128sts)
- 38th row: K
- 39th row: (K7, inc in next)x16 (144sts)
- Work 5 rows 1&1 rib
- Cast off loosely in rib

To make up: Stitch a length of wire to the WS of the pasty piece all around the base of the crimped edge where it meets the smooth knit. Be generous – don't pull the wire tight. Run wire around full circle, join by twisting ends together and bind sharp ends. Stuff with loose stuffing and fold pasty into shape. Stitch two halves together just above the wire. Pinch to make wavy edge. The wire will hold the shape.

For a child-friendly version without wire, fold pasty in half, sitting upright. Stuff with loose stuffing. Stitch sides together at base of crimped edge, pinching as you would with pastry. Vary the tension of the stiches to hold the wavy finish in place.

FLAT PASTY

- Work on 4 needles, joined in a circle
- Cast on 8
- 1st row: K
- 2nd row: Inc in every st   (16sts)
- Work 3 rows K
- 6th row: Inc in every st   (32sts)
- Work 5 rows K
- 12th row: Inc in every st   (64sts)
- Work 7 rows K
- 20th row: (Inc in next, K1)x32   (96sts)
- Work 5 rows K
- 26th row: (Inc in next, K2)x32 (128sts)
- Work 5 rows K
- 32nd row: (Inc in next, K3)x32 (160sts)
- Work 3 rows K
- Cast off loosely

DECORATIVE EDGING

- Work on 2 needles
- Cast on 9
- 1st row: K
- 2nd row: P6, turn –
- 3rd row: K6
- 4th row: P6, K3
- 5th row: K3, P6
- 6th row: K6, turn –
- 7th row: P6
- 8th row: K
- Repeat rows 1 to 8 (x23)
- Do not cast off – the length required depends on the size of the pasty.

To make up: Gently press pasty piece under damp cloth. Do not press the decorative edging. Cut out circle of wadding 1cm smaller than the pasty piece. Place the wadding on the WS of the knitted piece, add extra loose stuffing to form the pasty filling. Fold nearly in half so that the bottom is slightly proud of the top. Sew-up to close the pasty. Pin flat edge of trim to underside of pasty edge, stretching gently. Cast off edging trim now that length is confirmed. Stitch in place. Curve crimped edging over pasty, stitch in place through top and bottom of pasty.

TO COLOUR THE PASTIES

If using pastels, work in layers. Rub lightly with dry cloth between layers. Build colour gradually. Fix with spray fixative or hairspray.

If using paint, lightly dry-sponge colour in layers with thinned paint. Dab with dry cloth. Allow to dry between layers.

You will need

MATERIALS:
Colour Codes:
1 Sublime Baby Cashmerino Silk DK
(Shade 0278 – Cream)
2 Sublime Baby Cashmerino Silk DK
(Shade 0219 – Orange/Brown)
3 Patons 100% Cotton DK (Shade
2712 – Black) – For Collar

Black embroidery thread
Black beads for eyes
3 pipe cleaners
5 diamonds/beads to trim collar
Stuffing

NEEDLES:
Size 10/3.25mm
Darning needle

Bulldog Pup

The bulldog is a handsome, pugnacious animal, heavily muscled and with a very expressive face. They are generally very docile and need regular exercise but not too much. Their name originated from the sport of bull baiting, where the dog that managed to pin the bull to the ground by hanging onto its nose would be the winner. Bulldogs were therefore bred to be as muscular as possible with strong jaws and a ferocious temperament. Thankfully, bull baiting is no longer with us, but bulldogs are very much part of British folklore.

The bulldog was perhaps made most famous through its association with Winston Churchill during the Second World War. Churchill's appearance and stubborn never-say-die attitude invited comparison with the bulldog, long known for similar character traits. Indeed, the Russians and others came to refer to Churchill as the 'British Bulldog', and this characterisation did his reputation no harm in the depths of a fiercely fought war. The famous Karsh photograph of Churchill, taken in 1941 at a time when the war was not going well, shows bulldog spirit and demeanour at its finest. This photograph was taken after Churchill refused to remove his cigar, prompting Karsh to rather boldly walk up to the Prime Minister and snatch it. And the resulting bulldog glower became one of the most iconic photographs ever taken. Hopefully our bulldog also shows off just a little bit of that famous British spirit!

BODY

COLOUR 2

- Size 10/3.25mm needles

- Cast on 6
- Work 6 rows SS starting with K
- 7th row: K row – inc in 1st & last (8sts)
- Work 3 rows SS starting with P
- 11th row: Cast on 7, K15
- 12th row: Cast on 7, P22
- 13th row: K
- 14th row: P row – inc in 1st & last (24sts)
- 15th row: K
- 16th row: P row – inc in 1st & last (26sts)
- Work 4 rows SS starting with K
- 21st row: K row – inc in 1st & last (28sts)
- Work 3 rows SS starting with P
- 25th row: K4, inc in next, (K3, inc in next)×2, K2, inc in next, (K3, inc in next)×2, K4 (34sts)
- 26th row: P
- 27th row: K32, turn –
- 28th row: P30, turn –
- 29th row: K32
- 30th row: P (34sts)
- 31st row: K32, turn –
- 32nd row: P30, turn –
- 33rd row: K32 (34sts)
- 34th row: P34
- 35th row: K – inc in 1st, K31, turn –
- 36th row: P31, turn –
- 37th row: K33
- 38th row: P – inc in 1st, P34 (36sts)
- 39th row: K34, turn –
- 40th row: P32, turn –
- 41st row: K34 (36sts)
- 42nd row: P36
- 43rd row: K34, turn –
- 44th row: P32, turn –
- 45th row: K34

- 46th row: P36 (36sts)
- 47th row: K34, turn –
- 48th row: P32, turn –
- 49th row: K34 (36sts)
- 50th row: P36
- 51st row: K34, turn –
- 52d row: P32, turn –
- 53rd row: K34 (36sts)
- 54th row: P36
- 55th row: K34, turn –
- 56th row: P32, turn –
- 57th row: K34 (36sts)
- 58th row: P2tog, P32, P2tog (34sts)
- 59th row: K2tog, K30, K2tog (32sts)
- 60th row: P2tog, P28, P2tog (30sts)
- 61st row: Cast off 8, K2, K2tog, K5, K2tog, K2, cast off 8 (12sts)

TO CREATE HEAD

CHANGE TO COLOUR 1

- 62nd row: Cast on 4, K16, cast on 4 (20sts)
- 63rd row: P5, (inc in next, P1)×2, inc in next, inc in next, (P1, inc in next)×2, P5 (26sts)
- 64th row: K
- 65th row: P4, (inc in next, P1)×4, inc in next, inc in next, (P1, inc in next)×4, P4 (36sts)
- 66th row: K
- 67th row: P
- 68th row: K24, turn –
- 69th row: P12, turn –
- 70th row: K13, turn –
- 71st row: P14, turn –
- 72nd row: K13, turn –
- 73rd row: P12, turn –
- 74th row: K24 (36sts)
- Work 3 rows SS starting with P
- 78th row: K11, K2tog, K10, K2tog, K11 (34sts)
- 79th row: P
- 80th row: K12, K2tog, K1, K2tog, K2tog, K1, K2tog, K12 (30sts)

- 81st row: P
- 82nd row: K10, K2tog, K6, K2tog, K10 (28sts)
- 83rd row: P9, P2tog, P1, P2tog, P2tog, P1, P2tog, P9 (24sts)
- 84th row: K
- 85th row: P9, P2tog, P2, P2tog, P9 (22sts)
- 86th row: K7, inc in next, inc in next, K4, inc in next, inc in next, K7 (26sts)
- 87th row: P
- 88th row: K20, turn –
- 89th row: P14, turn –
- 90th row: K20 (26sts)
- Work 7 rows SS starting with P
- Thread all 26sts onto length of wool, doubled for strength. This forms the muzzle.
- Set aside.

GUSSET

COLOUR 1

- Size 9/3.75mm needles

- WORKING FROM NECK TO TAIL
- Cast on 8
- Work 6 rows SS starting with K
- 7th row: K1, inc in next, K4, inc in next, K1 (10sts)
- Work 13 rows SS starting with P
- 21st row: K2tog, K6, K2tog (8sts)
- Work 27 SS starting with P
- 49th row: K2tog, K4, K2tog (6sts)
- 50th row: P
- 51st row: K2tog, K2, K2tog (4sts)
- 52nd row: P
- 53rd row: K2tog, K2tog (2sts)
- 54th row: P
- Cast off

LEGS

COLOUR 1

- Size 10/3.25mm needles

FRONT LEGS – MAKE TWO

- Cast on 18
- Work 3 rows SS starting with K
- 4th row: P6, (P2tog)x3, P6   (15sts)
- 5th row: K5, cast off 5, K4   (10sts)
- 6th row: P, pulling 2 sides together
- Work 4 rows SS starting with K
- 11th row: (K1, inc in next)x2, K2, (inc in next, K1)x2   (14sts)
- Work 8 rows SS starting with P
- 20th row: P3, inc in next, P6, inc in next, P3   (16sts)
- Work 8 rows SS starting with K
- Cast off

BACK RIGHT LEG

- Cast on 18
- Work 3 rows SS starting with K
- 4th row: P4, P2tog, P2, P2tog, P2, P2tog, P4   (15sts)
- 5th row: K3, K2tog, K2tog, K1, K2tog, K2tog, K3   (11sts)
- 6th row: P4, P2tog, P5   (10sts)
- 7th row: K4, K2tog, K4   (9sts)
- Work 4 rows SS starting with P
- 12th row: P3, (inc in next)x3, P3   (12sts)
- Work 3 rows SS starting with K
- 16th row: P3, inc in next, P4, inc in next, P3   (14sts)
- Work 4 rows SS starting with K
- 21st row: K3, inc in next, K6, inc in next, K3   (16sts)
- Work 12 rows SS starting with P
- Cast off

BACK LEFT LEG

ABBREVIATIONS:

col – *Colour of yarn*

Work as for right leg rows 1 to 18

TO CREATE PATCH

- 19th row: K4 col 1, K1 col 2, K9 col 1
- 20th row: P8 col 1, P3 col 2, P3 col 1
- 21st row: K3 col 1, inc in next col 2, K3 col 2, K3 col 1, inc in next col 1, K3 col 1   (16sts)
- 22nd row: P8 col 1, P5 col 2, P3 col 1
- 23rd row: K3 col 1, K5 col 2, K8 col 1
- 24th row: P7 col 1, P7 col 2, P2 col 1
- 25th row: K2 col 1, K7 col 2, K7 col 1
- 26th row: P6 col 1, P8 col 2, P2 col 1
- 27th row: K2 col 1, K8 col 2, K6 col 1
- 28th row: P4 col 1, P11 col 2, P1 col 1
- 29th row: K1 col 1, K12 col 2, K3 col 1
- 30th row: P3 col 1, P12 col 2, P1 col 1
- 31st row: K2 col 1, K11 col 2, K3 col 1
- 32nd row: P5 col 1, P9 col 2, P2 col 1
- 33rd row: K2 col 1, K9 col 2, K5 col 1
- 34th row: P5 col 1, P9 col 2, P2 col 1
- 35th row: K3 col 1, K7 col 2, K6 col 1
- Cast off

EARS

LEFT EAR
COLOUR 1

- Size 10/3.25mm needles

- Cast on 8
- Work 4 rows SS starting with K
- 5th row: K1, inc in next, K4, inc in next, K1   (10sts)
- 6th row: P8, turn –
- 7th row: K8
- 8th row: P2tog, P8   (9sts)
- 9th row: K2tog, K5, K2tog   (7sts)
- 10th row: P
- 11th row: K2tog, K5   (6sts)
- 12th row: P
- 13th row: K2tog, K2, K2tog   (4sts)
- 14th row: P2tog, P2   (3sts)
- Pull wool through 3sts
- Tie off

RIGHT EAR
COLOUR 2

- Size 10/3.25mm needles

- Cast on 8
- Work 4 rows SS starting with P
- 5th row: P1, inc in next, P4, inc in next, P1   (10sts)
- 6th row: K8, turn –
- 7th row: P8
- 8th row: K8, K2tog   (9sts)
- 9th row: P2tog, P5, P2tog   (7sts)
- 10th row: K
- 11th row: P5, P2tog   (6sts)
- 12th row: K
- 13th row: P2tog, P2, P2tog   (4sts)
- 14th row: K2, K2tog
- Pull wool through 3sts
- Tie off

To make up: Lightly steam-press all pieces.

The dog's body and leg pieces are knitted extra-long so that each piece can be ruched to create folds in his fur. See photo for reference.

TO MAKE UP LEGS

With WS facing attach 3 drawstrings to each leg from ankle to top of leg – leave threads for ruching later. Sew-up small holes on top of front feet. Sew-up underside of paws to the ankle. Join back seams of each leg.
Cut one pipe cleaner to 22cm for pair of back legs, and one to 20cm for pair of front legs. Using one pipe cleaner per pair of legs, create a small circle in each end to form the pads of the feet. Insert inside the legs and push a small piece of wadding into each foot to pad-out. Bend pipe cleaner across the body, allowing for the back legs to be 5cm in height, front

legs to be 4cm in height. The pipe cleaner forms an upside-down U-shape. Ruche legs to fit length of pipe cleaner support and tie off drawstrings. The legs are not yet attached to any part of the body.

TO MAKE UP BODY

With WS facing attach 5 evenly spaced drawstrings parallel to the spine, from tail-end to neck-end of body piece. Ruche gently. Take third pipe cleaner, fold over one end by approx. 5cm and hook to the drawstring which is supporting the muzzle stitches. Secure the hook by twisting the pipe cleaner. Pull muzzle drawstring tight and tie off securely. Pull up muzzle to create squashed shape. The pipe cleaner should run the length of the dog from squashed muzzle to end of tail, approx. 16cm. Trim end of pipe cleaner and fold over to make safe. Attach pipe cleaner to end of tail. Catch body piece along the spine of the pipe cleaner in one or two places with loose stitches.

Sew-up the under-chin seam of head as far as the underside of the squashed muzzle – refer to photo for good shape. Stuff head.

Sew gusset into neck. Pin gusset to body seams, setting the leg pipe cleaners in position at front and back. When happy with shape, sew gusset seams from neck to tail, leaving an opening for stuffing. Once stuffed, sew up opening. Pull up the 'socks' of the legs. Stuff with a little wadding before attaching to the body as three-dimensional shapes.

Attach ears. Add black beads for eyes. Create nose with black embroidery thread.

Using pliers, bend the tail into shape. Bend back legs to kinked shape.

COLLAR

COLOUR 3

- Size 10/3.25mm needles

- Cast on 37
- Work 1 row
- Cast off

To make up: Attach diamonds/beads decoration. Place collar around neck. Stitch ends together.

Glossary

4 Ply – thickness of wool

DK – abbreviation for 'double knitting' (thickness of wool)

GS – abbreviation for 'garter stitch'; knit every row

i-cord – a process for knitting a tube or stalk or stem; with double-ended needles knit a row, slide the stitches to the other end of the needle (do not turn the knitting) knit the next row, pulling the yarn tight on the first stitch so that the knitting forms a tube, continue in this way until cord is desired length

inc – increase by knitting into the front and the back of the stitch 1 in 1 rib – K1, P1

K – abbreviation for 'knit'

K2tog – abbreviation for 'knit 2 stitches together'

MS – abbreviation for 'moss stitch'

P – abbreviation for 'purl'

P2tog – abbreviation for 'purl 2 stitches together'

psso – abbreviation for 'pass slip stitch over'; pass the slip stitch over the next stitch

Reverse SS – the same process as SS but the knobbly side is to the right side

RS – abbreviation for 'the right side of the work'

SS – abbreviation for 'stocking stitch'; alternate knit and purl rows, creating a smooth finish on one side, usually the right side

ssk – slip two stitches one at a time onto the right needle then knit them together

sl – abbreviation for 'slip'; slip the stitch onto the right needle without either knitting or purling it

st(s) – abbreviation for 'stitch' or 'stitches' if more than one

WS – abbreviation for 'the wrong side of the work'

yf – abbreviation for 'yarn forward'; bring the yarn from the back to the front of the work

yo – abbreviation for 'yarn over'; bring the yarn over the needle before working the next stitch

Hints and Tips

- The wools used in the patterns are listed; however, because we are working fairly small-scale you may choose to replace any suggested yarns with oddments you already have. Check that your yarn is of a similar weight/ply.

- All ends of wool should be finished off by weaving in before making up.

- Joining seams: To give a firm finish to seams, join using original weight of yarn, or for a softer finish and with very small pieces, pare yarn down.

- Pressing of knitted pieces: Generally these small items benefit from a gentle steam press before making up.
If you want to check the finish, knit a small square and test-press before starting one of the patterns.

- For a better fit: As every knitter works with a different tension you may wish to work up or down a size of needle.

- Stuffing heads & limbs: Try not to over- or under-stuff.
Bear in mind the finished character, and his or her shape.

- Heads & faces can be made more characterful by careful stuffing. To further define or alter a face shape, run a darning needle threaded with yarn through from one side to the other, pull gently and fasten off. Work from an image if possible, and look at shape of head – front, back and side views. Is there any feature that is particularly prominent? Using smaller amounts of stuffing at a time will give you more sensitive shaping.

Notes